Birds of New England

Todd Telander

FALCONGUIDES ®

GUILFORD, CONNECTICUT
HELENA, MONTANA

AN IMPRINT OF GLOBE PEQUOT PRESS

To my wife, Kirsten; my children, Miles and Oliver; and my parents,
all of whom have supported and encouraged me through the years.
Special thanks to Mike Denny for his expert critique of the illustrations.

To buy books in quantity for corporate use
or incentives, call **(800) 962-0973**
or e-mail **premiums@GlobePequot.com.**

FALCONGUIDES®

FalconGuides is an imprint of Globe Pequot Press.
Falcon, FalconGuides, and Outfit Your Mind are registered trademarks of
Morris Book Publishing, LLC.

Illustrations: Todd Telander
Project Editor: Staci Zacharski
Text Design: Sheryl P. Kober
Layout: Sue Murray

Library of Congress Cataloging-in-Publication Data is available on file.

ISBN 978-0-7627-8362-5

Printed in the United States of America

10 9 8 7 6 5 4 3 2 1

Contents

Passerines

Introduction

New England, the region of the United States that includes Maine, Vermont, New Hampshire, Massachusetts, Connecticut, and Rhode Island, is a region of vast diversity. It is bordered by the Appalachian Mountain chain on the west, Canada to the north, and the Atlantic Ocean to the east, and is marked by rolling hills, valleys, and lakes—remnants of the last glacial age. Mountainous coniferous forests, lush deciduous woodlands, grassy valleys, and varied coastline all provide habitat for a vast number and variety of bird species. Because of its position on the globe, New England finds itself host to visiting birds from the Arctic, the open Atlantic Ocean, and Europe, as well as those that come north from tropical areas. Whether you are searching for shearwaters off the coast, puffins on rocky cliffs, colorful warblers in groves of spruce, or cardinals in city parks, this guide describes 300 species you are likely to encounter here and should give you a good start to your birding exploration and enjoyment.

Notes about the Species Accounts

Order

The order of species listed in this guide is based on the most recent version of the *Checklist of North American Birds,* published by the American Ornithologists' Union. The arrangement of some groups, especially within the nonpasserines, may be slightly different than that of older field guides but reflects the most recent accepted arrangement.

Names

Both the common name and the scientific name are included for each entry. Of the two, the universally accepted scientific name of genus and species is the more reliable identifier because common names can vary by region and sometimes there may be more than one. Also, if you know a little Latin, you can often learn interesting facts about a bird from its Latin name. For instance, the wood thrush's scientific name, *Hylocichla mustelina,* derives from the Latin *hylocichal,* meaning "of the forest," and *mustelina,* referring to the weasel-like color of its plumage.

Families

Birds are grouped into families based on similar traits, behaviors, and genetics. When trying to identify an unfamiliar bird, it can often be helpful to first place it into a family, which will reduce your search to a smaller group. For birds with which you are already familiar, try to understand what makes them fit into their particular family. Characteristics like bill size and shape, feeding behavior, and habitat preference can be remarkably consistent within a family. Then when you encounter an unfamiliar bird, you can make a pretty good guess as to which group it belongs to (or doesn't!).

Size

The size given for each bird is the average length from the tip of the bill to the end of the tail if the bird was laid out flat. Sometimes females and males vary in size, and this variation is described in the text. Size can be misleading if you are looking at a small bird that happens to have a very long tail or bill. It can be more effective to judge the bird's relative size by comparing the size difference between two or more species.

Season

The season given in the accounts is the time when the greatest number of individuals occur in New England. Some species are year-round residents, some may spend only summers or winters here, and some may be transient, only stopping during the spring or fall migration. Even if only part of the year is indicated for a species, be aware that there may be individuals that arrive earlier or remain for longer than the given time frame. Plumage also changes with the season for many birds, and this is indicated in the text and illustrations.

Habitat

A bird's habitat is one of the first clues to its identification. Note the environment (including vegetation, climate, elevation, substrate, presence or absence of water) where you see a bird and compare it with the description listed. This can be especially helpful when identifying a bird that shares traits with related species. For example, cattle egrets and snowy egrets are similar in appearance, but cattle egrets are found in drier fields and pastures, while snowy egrets prefer swamps and open water.

Illustrations

The illustrations show the adult bird in the plumage most likely to be encountered during the season(s) it is in New England. If it is likely that you will find more than one type of plumage during this time, the alternate plumage is also shown. For birds that are sexually dimorphic (females and males look different), illustrations of both sexes are usually included. Other plumages, such as those of juveniles and alternate morphs, are described in the text.

Bird Topography and Terms

Bird topography describes the outer surface of a bird and how various anatomical structures fit together. Below is a diagram outlining the terms most commonly used to describe the feathers and bare parts of a bird.

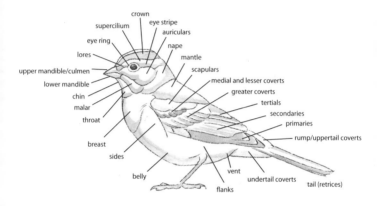

NONPASSERINES

Greater White-fronted Goose, *Anser albifrons*
Family Anatidae (Geese, Ducks, Mergansers)
Size: Large but highly variable; 28"
Season: Winter
Habitat: Swamps, marshy areas, coastal fields

The greater white-fronted goose is a medium-size goose that breeds in the Arctic and migrates through New England on its way to southern wintering grounds. Its plumage is grayish brown above and on the head and neck, while its tail coverts and terminal tail band are white. The breast and flanks are barred with brown and black, and the bill is pinkish, bordered at the base by white along the front of the face (lacking in juveniles). The upper portions of the flanks form a thin white line. These geese forage for a variety of plants or small invertebrates in marshes or nearby fields. The adult is illustrated.

Snow Goose, *Chen caerulescens*
Family Anatidae (Ducks, Geese, Mergansers)
Size: 28"
Season: Winter
Habitat: Grasslands, marshes

Traveling in huge, impressive flocks, the snow goose visits New England to spend the winter after breeding in the Arctic tundra. It has two color forms: the "blue" and the more common "white." The white form is predominantly white with black outer wing feathers and a pale yellowish wash to the face during summer. The blue form retains the white head and lower belly but is otherwise dark slate gray or brownish gray. In both morphs its bill is pink, thick at the base, and has a black patch where the mandibles meet. The legs of both types are pink. Snow geese feed mostly on the ground, eating shoots, roots, grains, and insects. The similar Ross's goose is smaller and has a shorter bill. The adult is illustrated.

Brant, *Branta bernicla*
Family Anatidae (Geese, Ducks, Mergansers)
Size: 25.5"
Season: Winter
Habitat: Coastal bays, marshes or nearby fields

The brant is a small, dark, fairly short-necked goose with a short, stubby bill. Its plumage is barred sooty gray above with black flight feathers. Its underparts are mixed gray and white down to the flanks, then become pure white to the short, black-edged tail. The head and neck are black with a partial white neck band (lacking in juveniles). Although western populations are quite dark on the breast, here in the East the breast is pale with obvious separation between the lower neck and the breast. Sexes are similar. Brant feed in the water for eelgrass and aquatic invertebrates or in nearby fields for insects and emit a low, throaty, croaking call. They fly low to the ground in rather loose, unorganized groups. The adult is illustrated.

Canada Goose, *Branta canadensis*
Family Anatidae (Geese, Ducks, Mergansers)
Size: 27"–35", depending on race
Season: Winter
Habitat: Marshes, grasslands, public parks, golf courses

A common goose, the Canada Goose comprises several subspecies—fewer since a reclassification placed some of its smaller members under the cackling goose. Often found in suburban settings, this vegetarian bird forages on land for grass, seeds, and grain, or in the water, upending like the dabbling ducks for aquatic vegetation. It has a heavy body with short, thick legs and a long neck. Overall it is barred gray brown with a white rear, short black tail, black neck, and a white patch running under the neck to behind the eyes. During its powerful flight in the classic V formation, the white across the rump makes a semicircular patch between the tail and back. Its voice is a loud honk. The adult is illustrated.

Tundra Swan, *Cygnus columbianus*
Family Anatidae (Geese, Ducks, Mergansers)
Size: 52"
Season: Spring–fall
Habitat: Coastal estuaries, shallow lakes

The tundra swan is America's most widespread swan and also the smallest, wintering along coastal areas of North America and nesting in the tundra of the far north. It is white overall, sometimes stained with brown, except for a black bill and legs. The bill shows a variable-size patch of yellow just in front of the eye, or this area may be completely black. The tundra swan has a long neck and long body, a forehead and crown that are quite rounded, and an upper mandible that has a slightly concave profile. Juveniles are dusky gray with a pinkish bill. They forage for aquatic plants and animals, either on the ground or in the water. The adult is illustrated.

Mute Swan, *Cygnus olor*
Family Anatidae (Geese, Ducks, Mergansers)
Size: 60"
Season: Year-round
Habitat: Ponds, lakes, coastal bays;
usually in or near developed areas

Native to northern Europe and central Asia, the mute swan was introduced in the early 1900s to parks and gardens of the eastern United States. It is a large, graceful swan that holds its neck in a smooth curve and has a relatively long, pointed tail and uniformly white plumage. The face is black in front of the eyes, meeting with a reddish-orange bill and a black, bulbous knob at the forehead. Although mostly quiet, it is capable of a range of hisses, snorts, and loud, nasal calls. Mute swans forage for aquatic plants and can be quite aggressive, often displaying a posture with the head tilted down and the wings raised over the back. It is a species of concern because as its range expands, it displaces many native birds. The adult is illustrated.

Wood Duck, *Aix sponsa*
Family Anatidae (Geese, Ducks, Mergansers)
Size: 18"
Season: Year-round
Habitat: Wooded ponds and swamps

The regal wood duck is among the dabbling ducks, or those that tip headfirst into shallow water to pluck aquatic plants and animals from the bottom. The male is long tailed and small billed and shows a dark back, light buff flanks, and sharp black-and-white head patterning. It also sports a bushy head crest that droops behind the nape. The female is gray brown with spotting along the underside and a conspicuous white teardrop-shaped eye patch. Both sexes swim with their heads angled downward as if in a nod and have sharp claws, which they use to cling to branches and snags. The breeding female (top) and breeding male (bottom) are illustrated.

American Wigeon, *Anas americana*
Family Anatidae (Geese, Ducks, Mergansers)
Size: 19"
Season: Winter
Habitat: Shallow ponds, fields

The American wigeon is also known as the baldpate, in reference to its white crown. A wary and easily alarmed duck, it feeds on the water's surface, often gleaning prey stirred up by the efforts of diving ducks. The underside is a light cinnamon color with white undertail coverts, and the back is light brown. The male has a white crown and forehead with a very slight crest when seen in profile and a glossy dark-green patch extending from the eye to the back of the neck. A white wing covert patch can usually be seen on the folded wing but is more obvious in flight. The head of the female is unmarked and brownish. The breeding female (top) and breeding male (bottom) are illustrated.

Gadwall, *Anas strepera*
Family Anatidae (Geese, Ducks, Mergansers)
Size: 20.5"
Season: Year-round
Habitat: Shallow lakes, marshes

The gadwall is a buoyant, plain-colored dabbling duck with a steep forehead and a somewhat angular head. The breeding male is grayish overall with very fine variegation and barring. The rump and undertail coverts are black, the scapulars are light orange brown, the tertials are gray, and the head is lighter below the eye and darker above. Females and nonbreeding males are a mottled brown with few distinguishing markings. In flight there is a distinctive white speculum (inner wing patch) that is most prominent in males. Gadwalls dabble or dive for a variety of aquatic plants and invertebrates and often gather in large flocks away from the shore. The breeding female (top) and breeding male (bottom) are illustrated.

Mallard, *Anas platyrhynchos*
Family Anatidae (Geese, Ducks, Mergansers)
Size: 23"
Season: Year-round
Habitat: Virtually any water environment, parks, urban areas

The ubiquitous mallard is the most abundant duck in the Northern Hemisphere. It is a classic dabbling duck, plunging its head into the water with its tail up, searching for aquatic plants, animals, and snails, although it will also eat worms, seeds, insects, and even mice. Noisy and quacking, it is heavy but is a strong flier. The male has a dark head with green or blue iridescence, a white neck ring, and a large yellow bill. The underparts are pale, with a chestnut-brown breast. The female is plain brownish with buff scalloped markings, a dark eye line, and an orangey bill with a dark center. The speculum is blue on both sexes, and the tail coverts often curl upward. Mallards form huge floating flocks called "rafts." To achieve flight, it lifts straight into the air without running. The breeding female (top) and breeding male (bottom) are illustrated.

American Black Duck, *Anas rubripes*
Family Anatidae (Geese, Ducks, Mergansers)
Size: 23"
Season: Year-round
Habitat: Lakes, ponds, saltwater and freshwater marshes, estuaries

The American Black Duck is easily overlooked because of its similarity to the female mallard. It is shaped just like a mallard, with a robust body and large bill, and shares the same dabbling behavior when feeding, probing for aquatic plants and invertebrates with its tail end pointed up out of the water. Overall, however, American black ducks are darker, an overall deep gray-brown, with only thin, paler edges to the flank and mantle feathers. The head and neck are paler gray with a dark eye stripe. Males and females are similar, but males have a light yellow-green bill while females have a dark, olive-green bill. In flight note the highly contrasting underwings and the deep-blue speculum, which has no white border. The adult is illustrated here.

Northern Shoveler,
Anas clypeata
Family Anatidae (Geese, Ducks, Mergansers)
Size: 19"
Season: Summer
Habitat: Shallow marshes, lakes, bays

Also known as the spoonbill duck, the Northern Shoveler skims the surface of the water with its neck extended, scooping up aquatic animals and plants with its long, shovel-like bill. It will also suck up the ooze from mud and strain it through bristles at the edge of its bill, retaining worms, leeches, and snails. This medium-size duck seems top-heavy due to its large bill. The male has a dark-green head, gray bill, large chestnut side patches, and white underside plumage. The female is pale brownish overall with an orangish bill. The breeding female (top) and breeding male (bottom) are illustrated.

Northern Pintail, *Anas acuta*
Family Anatidae
(Geese, Ducks, Mergansers)
Size: 21"
Season: Year-round
Habitat: Marshes, shallow lakes,
coastal bays

Among the most abundant ducks in North America, the Northern Pintail is an elegant, slender dabbling duck with a long neck, small head, and narrow wings. In breeding plumage the male has long, pointed central tail feathers. It is gray along the back and sides with a brown head and a white breast. A white stripe extends from the breast along the back of the neck. The female has a light brown head and is mottled brown and tan overall. To feed, the northern pintail bobs its head into the water to capture aquatic invertebrates and plants from the muddy bottom. It rises directly out of the water to take flight. The breeding female (top) and breeding male (bottom) are illustrated.

Green-winged Teal,
Anas crecca
Family Anatidae
(Geese, Ducks, Mergansers)
Size: 14"
Season: Year-round
Habitat: Marshes, ponds

The green-winged teal is a cute, very small, active duck with a small, thin bill. The breeding male is silvery gray with a dotted, tawny breast patch, a pale-yellow hip patch, and a distinct vertical white bar on its side. The head is rusty brown with an iridescent-green patch around and behind the eye. Females and nonbreeding males are mottled brown with a dark eye line and white belly. Green-winged teals dabble in the shallows for plant material and small invertebrates. They are quick and agile in flight and sport a bright-green speculum. They form very large winter flocks. The breeding female (top) and breeding male (bottom) are illustrated.

Blue-winged Teal, *Anas discors*
Family Anatidae (Geese, Ducks, Mergansers)
Size: 16"
Season: Summer
Habitat: Freshwater marshes and mudflats, wet agricultural areas

Often seen in large flocks, the blue-winged teal, also known as the white-faced teal, is a small duck that skims the water surface for aquatic plants and invertebrates. The male is mottled brown below, with a prominent white patch near the hip area, and is dark above, with gray on the head and a white vertical crescent at the base of the bill. The female is brownish, with scalloped flanks and a plain head with a dark eye line, and is pale at the lores. Both sexes have a light-blue wing patch visible in flight. The breeding female (top) and breeding male (bottom) are illustrated.

Canvasback,
Aythya valisineria
Family Anatidae (Geese, Ducks, Mergansers)
Size: 21"
Season: Winter
Habitat: Grassy wetlands, lakes

The canvasback is a stocky, thick-necked diving duck with a long, shallow forehead that slopes into the angle of the bill. The middle section of the breeding male, including back, wings, and belly, is entirely white. The tail and breast are black, and the head is a rusty brown that is darker on the crown and front of the face. The eye is deep red. The female is very pale overall, with a light, canvas-colored back and a tan head and neck. The canvasback runs across the water to take flight, whereupon its light middle and darker ends are striking. It usually feeds by diving for aquatic plants. The breeding male is illustrated.

Redhead, *Aythya americana*
Family Anatidae (Geese, Ducks, Mergansers)
Size: 19"
Season: Fall–spring
Habitat: Shallow lakes, marshes

The redhead is a heavy-bodied diving duck with a steep forehead and a large, rounded head. The breeding male is pale gray, with a dark rear end and breast. The head is light rusty brown, the eye is yellow, and the bill is bluish with a black tip. The female is brownish gray overall with pale areas at the base of the bill and throat. In both sexes the upper side of the wing has white flight feathers and dark-gray coverts. These birds run across the water to become airborne. They forage by diving for aquatic plants and invertebrate and may form huge floating "rafts" during the winter. Redheads are similar in pattern to the larger canvasbacks. The breeding female (top) and breeding male (bottom) are illustrated.

Ring-necked Duck, *Aythya collaris*
Family Anatidae (Geese, Ducks, Mergansers)
Size: 17"
Season: Year-round
Habitat: Shallow lakes and ponds near woodlands, coastal bays

The ring-necked duck, also known as the ring-billed duck, is in the group of diving ducks that typically swim underwater to find plant and animal prey, although it may also behave like a dabbling duck and bob for food at the surface. This gregarious small duck looks tall with its postlike head and neck and peaked crown. The breeding male is stunning, with contrasting light and dark plumage and a dark metallic-brown-purple head. The bill is gray with a white ring and black tip, and the base of the bill is edged with white feathers. The female is more brownish overall, with a white eye ring. The ring around the neck, for which this duck is named, is actually a very inconspicuous brownish band at the bottom of the neck in the male bird. The breeding female (top) and breeding male (bottom) are illustrated.

Lesser Scaup, *Aythya affinis*
Family Anatidae (Geese, Ducks, Mergansers)
Size: 17"
Season: Fall–spring
Habitat: Marshes, shallow lakes, coastal bays

The lesser scaup is a small, short-bodied duck with a tall head profile and a relatively thin bill. The breeding male is distinctly two-toned, with white sides, a variegated pale-gray back, and a black rear and front. The head has a dark metallic-violet or greenish cast in good light, and the bill has a small black dot at the nail. The nonbreeding male is paler with brown on the sides. The female is gray brown with a dark-brown head and a white patch at the base of the bill. This is a diving duck that forages for aquatic plants and insects. It is very similar to the greater scaup but is smaller and has a more peaked head. The breeding female (top) and breeding male (bottom) are illustrated.

King Eider, *Somateria spectabilis*

Family Anatidae (Geese, Ducks, Mergansers)
Size: 21.5"
Season: Winter
Habitat: Inshore coastal waters

The king eider is a handsome sea-duck of the far north that visits New England in the winter. It has a short neck and a long, flattened head that merges into a bright-orange frontal protuberance, and a small, reddish bill. The head is further ornamented with powder blue on the crown and nape, green on the cheeks, and a dark line through the eye and outlining the base of the bill. The body is black except for the white breast, upperwing coverts, and a lower flank patch. The nonbreeding male is mostly dark brown with a much-reduced bill lobe. Females are brownish, extensively mottled, and scalloped with dark brown. King eiders dive, often very deep, for small aquatic prey and plants. The female (top) and breeding male (bottom) are illustrated.

Common Eider,

Somateria mollissima
Family Anatidae (Geese, Ducks, Mergansers)
Size: 21.5"
Season: Year-round
Habitat: Rocky coastline (summer); open coastal waters (winter)

The common eider is the largest duck in North America. It is a stocky, short-necked duck with a distinctive sloping forehead profile. The male in breeding plumage is crisp white above, black below, with a black tail and flight feathers. The head is capped with black, the nape is pale green, the bill is bright yellow, and there is a thin black strip under the chin. Nonbreeding males become dark on the head, breast, and back. Females are extensively mottled brownish overall with a gray bill. Common eiders dive for fish, crustaceans, and other aquatic invertebrates. The female (top) and breeding male (bottom) are illustrated.

Surf Scoter, *Melanitta perspicillata*
Family Anatidae
(Geese, Ducks, Mergansers)
Size: 20"
Season: Winter
Habitat: Coastal waters

The surf scoter is a stocky, large-headed, coastal diving duck with short, pointed wings and a thick-based, colorful bill. The male is black overall with white patches at the back of the neck and on the forehead. The eyes are light, and the bill is orange with white sides framing a round black spot. The female is brownish overall with a black cap, grayish bill, and faint white patches along the base of the bill and cheeks and sometimes on the nape. Surf scoters dive for shellfish and crustaceans, propelled by their short wings. Because of their markings, they are sometimes called skunk-headed ducks. The breeding female (top) and breeding male (bottom) are illustrated.

White-winged Scoter,
Melanitta fusca
Family Anatidae (Geese, Ducks,
Mergansers)
Size: 21"
Season: Winter
Habitat: Coastal waters and bays

The white-winged scoter, which is the largest scoter, is sometimes called the velvet scoter because of its smooth, dark plumage. The male is brownish black overall with a distinctive white patch on the inner wing (speculum) and white, crescent-shaped spots behind the eyes. The concave forehead meets the orange bill with a small, black knob. Females are similar but have fuzzy, pale spots at the ears and lores and a straighter, gray bill. White-winged scoters favor crustaceans, especially mussels, in the rocky intertidal zone. The female (top) and breeding male (bottom) are illustrated.

Harlequin Duck,
Histrionicus histrionicus
Family Anatidae (Geese, Ducks, Mergansers)
Size: 16.5"
Season: Winter
Habitat: Rocky coastal surf zone

The harlequin duck is a graceful, small sea duck at home in rough coastal waters or rushing mountain streams. The breeding male is slate gray overall with bright chestnut flanks and contrasting white markings along the back, breast, and head. Nonbreeding males are brownish overall with much-reduced white markings; females resemble nonbreeding males but with white marks restricted to the belly, front of the face, and a spot at the ear. As harlequin ducks dive, they use their feet and wings to catch fish and aquatic invertebrates, and fly low over the water with rapid wing beats. The female (top) and breeding male (bottom) are illustrated.

Long-tailed Duck,
Clangula hyemalis
Family Anatidae (Geese, Ducks, Mergansers)
Size: 16" (female), 21" (male)
Season: Winter
Habitat: Offshore coastal waters

Also known as the old-squaw, the long-tailed duck is a small sea duck with distinctive, long, thin central tail feathers (in males). The winter male is boldly patterned white and black with silvery gray scapulars and flanks and a broad black breast band. The head is white with a gray face and darker cheek patch, white eye ring, and two-toned black-and-pink bill. The female is dark brown above and on the breast, with a white face and black crown. When summering in the far north and Alaska, its plumage becomes darker. Propelled by wings and feet, long-tailed ducks dive deep into the water (up to 200 feet) in search of marine invertebrates and plants. They voice a collection of noisy clucks or a loud, far-reaching yodel. The female (top) and winter male (bottom) are illustrated.

Bufflehead, *Bucephala albeola*
Family Anatidae (Geese, Ducks,
Mergansers)
Size: 14"
Season: Winter
Habitat: Lakes, rivers, coastal bays

The bufflehead is diminutive; indeed, it is the smallest duck in North America. Also known as the bumblebee duck, this small diver forms small flocks that forage in the open water for aquatic plants and invertebrates. The puffy, rounded head seems large for its body and small gray-blue bill. The breeding male is striking, with a large white patch on the back half of its head that contrasts with the black front of the head and back. The underside is white. The female is paler overall with a dark gray-brown head and an airfoil-shaped white patch behind the eye. The bufflehead flies low to the water with rapid wing beats. The breeding female (top) and breeding male (bottom) are illustrated.

Common Goldeneye,
Bucephala clangula
Family Anatidae
(Geese, Ducks, Mergansers)
Size: 18.5"
Season: Year-round
Habitat: Lakes, rivers, coastal areas

The common goldeneye is a compact, large-headed diving duck with a tall, rounded head and stubby bill. The breeding male shows stark color contrasts, with its white body streaked above with black, black rear, and greenish-black head. It has bright-yellow eyes and circular white patches between the eyes and bill. The female is gray overall with a brown head and a yellow-tipped bill. This duck is sometimes called the "whistler" because of the whistling sound made by its wings in flight. In the winter it can be found in small flocks. The breeding female (top) and breeding male (bottom) are illustrated.

Hooded Merganser,
Lophodytes cucullatus
Family Anatidae
(Geese, Ducks, Mergansers)
Size: 18"
Season: Year-round
Habitat: Lakes, ponds, coastal waters

The mergansers are known as the fishing ducks or sawtooths. The hooded merganser is a small merganser with a small, thin bill, a long tail, and a dramatic crest. The males are black above and orange brown below with a white breast divided by vertical black stripes. The long tertials are striped with white. The male's crest can be low or raised to be tall and rounded and shows a clean white patch behind the bright-yellow eye. Females are grayish brown, lighter below, and have a rusty-brown crest that is much shorter than the male's and fans out to the back. Nonbreeding males are similar to females. Hooded mergansers dive underwater for fish, amphibians, and invertebrates. The female (top) and breeding male (bottom) are illustrated.

Common Merganser,
Mergus merganser
Family Anatidae (Geese, Ducks, Mergansers)
Size: 25"
Season: Year-round
Habitat: Lakes, rivers, coastal bays

The common merganser is a long, sleek diving duck with a rounded head and a long, thin bill. The breeding male is dark gray above and white (sometimes washed with pale brown) below. The head is black with a metallic-green sheen, and the bill is red with a dark tip. The female is similar to the nonbreeding male, being gray overall with a rusty-brown head and a white chin and neck. Also known as the sawtooth, the common merganser dives for fish or aquatic invertebrates and grips its prey with the sawlike serrations on its bill. It runs across the water to take off, but its flight is fast and direct. The breeding female (top) and breeding male (bottom) are illustrated.

Red-breasted Merganser,
Mergus serrator
Family Anatidae
(Geese, Ducks, Mergansers)
Size: 23"
Season: Year-round
Habitat: Coastal wetlands, bays

The red-breasted merganser is another merganser of New England that dives and chases fish of considerable size underwater and secures its catch with a long, thin bill that is serrated along the edges. Both male and female red-breasted mergansers sport a fine, long, two-part crest. The male has a white band around its neck, dark head, red bill, and gray flanks. The female is grayish overall with a brown head. The nonbreeding male closely resembles the female. Flight is low and quick on pointed wings. The female (top) and breeding male (bottom) are illustrated.

Ruddy Duck, *Oxyura jamaicensis*
Family Anatidae (Geese, Ducks, Mergansers)
Size: 15"
Season: Fall–spring
Habitat: Coastal waters, wetlands, rivers

The ruddy duck is a member of the "stiff-tailed ducks," known for their rigid tail feathers, which are often cocked up in display. It dives deep into the water for its food, which consists of aquatic vegetation, and flies low over the water with quick wing beats. This relatively small duck has a big head and a flat, broad body. The breeding male is a rich sienna brown overall with white cheeks, a black cap and nape, and a bright-blue bill. The female is drab with a conspicuous dark stripe across the cheek. Nonbreeding males become gray. The ruddy duck can sink low into the water, grebe-like, and will often dive to escape danger. The breeding female (top) and breeding male (bottom) are illustrated.

Gray Partridge, *Perdix perdix*
Family Phasianidae
(Pheasants, Grouse, Turkeys)
Size: 13"
Season: Year-round
Habitat: Open grasslands and agricultural fields

The gray partridge is a chunky, ground-dwelling game bird that has been introduced from Asia and is fairly uncommon in New England. It has a stubby, gray bill, rounded wings, and a short tail. The plumage is mottled in tones of grayish brown, with rufous tones on the head, along the flanks, and on the outer tail feathers. A dark-brown patch of variable size occurs on the belly (most prominently in males). Its flight is usually restricted to short bursts, and it often travels on foot in small groups (coveys) of up to a dozen or so. Gray partridges forage on the ground for seeds and voice a high-pitched, grating, raspy call. The adult male is illustrated.

Ring-necked Pheasant,
Phasianus colchicus
Family Phasianidae (Pheasants, Grouse, Turkeys)
Size: Male 21", female to 34"
Season: Year-round
Habitat: Grasslands, woodland edges, agricultural land with brushy cover

Another introduced species, the ring-necked pheasant is a large, beautifully colored, chicken-shaped bird with a very long, pointed tail. The male is ornately patterned in rufous, gold, and blue gray, with pale spotting on the wings and back and dark spotting underneath. The head is dark iridescent green blue with extensive red facial skin and a tufted crown. There is a clean white ring about the neck. The female is much plainer, mottled brown above and plain below, without obvious head markings. Ring-necked pheasants peck on the ground for seeds, grasses, and insects. Sounds include a harsh, two-syllabled *auk-CAW* vocalization and muffled wing fluttering. They are strong runners and fliers. The adult male is illustrated.

Ruffed Grouse, *Bonasa umbellus*
Family Phasianidae (Pheasants, Grouse, Turkeys)
Size: 17"
Season: Year-round
Habitat: Mixed mountainous woodlands

The ruffed grouse is a cryptically colored ground bird with a thick body, rounded wings, longish tail, and small head that is often peaked in a triangular crest. Two color morphs appear: gray and rufous. The gray morph is mottled gray and brown above and on the head and shows black-and-white spotting. The underside is white, heavily barred with black. Males have a black ruff about the neck that is held erect during display behaviors. Both sexes have a dark, subterminal tail band (often incomplete in females). Rufous morphs are similar but are cast overall with rufous tones. Ruffed grouse feed on the ground or in trees for seeds, berries, and buds. Their most distinctive sound is a repeated low, muffled whoompf, increasing in tempo, that the male bird produces by pumping its wings together. The adult male (gray morph) is illustrated.

Spruce Grouse, *Falcipennis canadensis*
Family Phasianidae (Pheasants, Grouse, Turkeys)
Size: 15.5"
Season: Year-round
Habitat: Mixed coniferous or spruce woodlands and clearings, particularly of inland subalpine regions

The spruce grouse is a compact, plump, docile ground bird with a comparatively short tail, short neck, and small bill. Two groups of this species exist, differing by tail pattern and amount of white plumage, but only one group is found in New England. The male is mottled brown and black across the back and wings and has a black, rufous-tipped tail, black neck, and black breast patch. The underside and flanks are dark with extensive white spots and streaks, while the head is blackish with bright-red eye combs and thin white markings under the eyes and at the cheeks. Females are well-camouflaged in mottled tones of brown, black, rust, and white. Spruce grouse feed on the ground or low in trees for leaves, needles, berries, and insects. During spring males strut in open areas with their tails outspread. The adult male is illustrated.

Wild Turkey, *Meleagris gallopavo*
Family Phasianidae (Pheasants, Grouse, Turkeys)
Size: 36"–48"; male larger than female
Season: Year-round
Habitat: Open mixed woodlands

The wild turkey is a very large (though slimmer than the domestic variety), dark, ground-dwelling bird. The legs are thick and stout, and the heavily barred plumage is quite iridescent in strong light. The head and neck appear small for the body size and are covered with bluish, warty, crinkled bare skin that droops under the chin in a red wattle. Often foraging in flocks, wild turkeys roam the ground for seeds, grubs, and insects and then roost at night in trees. Males emit the familiar gobble, while females are less vocal, making a soft clucking sound. In display, the male will hunch with its tail up and spread like a giant fan, revealing a white terminal band. The adult male is illustrated.

Northern Bobwhite,
Colinus virginianus
Family Odontophoridae (Quail)
Size: 10"
Season: Year-round
Habitat: Brushy fields and open woodlands

The bobwhite, like other quail, is a secretive, ground-dwelling bird that usually takes flight only if alarmed. It travels in coveys of ten or more, while scavenging for seeds, berries, and insects. It is plump with a very short, gray tail and a short, thick, curved bill. Its plumage is heavily streaked rufous, gray, and black, with a plain, rufous breast below a mottled black upper neck. It has a white superciliary stripe and throat. The female is paler with a greater extent of rufous coloring and a buffy eye line and throat. Its call sounds somewhat like its name, *bob-white*. The adult male is illustrated.

Red-throated Loon,
Gavia stellata
Family Gaviidae (Loons)
Size: 25"
Season: Winter
Habitat: Coastal bays, estuaries

The red-throated loon, North America's smallest loon, has a thin, pointed bill that it habitually holds at an upward-tilted angle. The breeding adult is dark with white mottling above and is white below. The head is pale gray with a rust throat patch and black-and-white striping down the nape. The bill is black. The non-breeding adult has a head that is dark above the eye and white across the face and foreneck. Its bill is pale gray and it lacks the throat patch. Red-throated loons dive deep underwater in search of fish, propelled by their strong, webbed feet. In flight they hold their heads outstretched below the line of the body and on land are quite clumsy. The nonbreeding adult (top) and breeding adult (bottom) are illustrated.

Common Loon, *Gavia immer*

Family Gaviidae (Loons)
Size: 24"
Season: Year-round
Habitat: Coastal waters,
inland lakes

Riding low in the water outside the surf zone, this heavy waterbird periodically dives for fish, propelled by its strong webbed feet. Designed for a life in the water, it has legs set far back on its body, which makes walking on land a clumsy affair and takeoff into the air labored. In the winter this bird has drab, gray-and-white plumage, unlike the flashy black-and-white spotted plumage it sports during the summer in northern lakes. Its call is a haunting yodel but not commonly heard while here for the winter months. In winter common loons are often seen scattered singly or in pairs along the coast. The breeding adult (top) and nonbreeding adult (bottom) are illustrated.

Pied-billed Grebe,

Podilymbus podiceps
Family Podicipedidae (Grebes)
Size: 13"
Season: Year-round
Habitat: Freshwater ponds and lakes

The pied-billed grebe is a secretive, small grebe that lurks in sheltered waters diving for small fish, leeches, snails, and crawfish. When alarmed, or to avoid predatory snakes and hawks, it has the habit of sinking until only its head is above water, remaining that way until danger has passed. It is brownish overall and slightly darker above, with a tiny tail and short wings. The breeding adult has a conspicuous dark ring around the middle of the bill, which is missing in winter plumage. Pied-billed grebes nest on a floating mat of vegetation. The breeding adult is illustrated.

Horned Grebe, *Podiceps auritus*
Family Podicipedidae (Grebes)
Size: 14"
Season: Fall through spring
Habitat: Coastal bays, inland marshes and lakes

The horned grebe is a sleek, compact, relatively heavy waterbird with a short, straight bill. Like other grebes, it has heavily lobed feet placed far to the back of its body, which it uses to swim rapidly underwater after fish. The breeding adult is slate gray on the back with rufous flanks and neck and a white belly. A patch of golden-yellow feathers plume back behind the eye (creating the "horn") and are bordered by a black crown and upper neck. Nonbreeding adults are grayish above, streaked gray on the flanks, and have a white foreneck. Their heads are dark gray above the eye and white across the face. All plumages show a pale tip to the bill. In flight horned grebes hold their upper bodies and head at an upward angle. The nonbreeding adult (top) and breeding adult (bottom) are illustrated.

Red-necked Grebe,
Podiceps grisegena
Family Podicipedidae (Grebes)
Size: 18"
Season: Winter
Habitat: Coastal bays, inland marshes, and lakes

The red-necked grebe is a fairly large grebe with a long, pointed bill that is usually held tilted down. The breeding plumage is dark gray above and white below, with a rufous neck, whitish face, and a black cap. There are white patches on the leading and trailing edges of the inner wings that are most noticeable in flight. The lower half of the bill is distinctly yellow. In winter the neck and face become pale gray. Red-necked grebes dive underwater for fish and other aquatic animals, create floating nests of vegetation, and carry their young chicks on their backs. The nonbreeding adult (top) and breeding adult (bottom) are illustrated.

Northern Fulmar,
Fulmarus glacialis
Family Procellariidae (Fulmars,
Shearwaters)
Size: 18.5"
Season: Winter
Habitat: Offshore waters

The northern fulmar is a member of the "tubenose" family, with a stubby, thick bill topped with a short tube to aid in salt excretion. It is superficially similar to a gull but is distinguished by the bill shape, steep forehead, thick neck, and its tendency to fly on flat wings. The plumage can be of a light, dark, or intermediate phase. Birds in light-phase plumage are white with a mottled gray back and upper wing and a dark tail. Dark-phase plumage is uniformly gray. Northern fulmars scavenge food from the water's surface, often following fishing vessels, and hold their bill at a distinct downward tilt. The adult is illustrated.

Great Shearwater,
Puffinus gravis
Family Procellariidae (Fulmars, Shearwaters)
Size: 18"
Season: Spring–fall
Habitat: Open ocean

The great shearwater is a large, strong shearwater with long, pointed wings and a relatively narrow, tube-nosed bill. Its plumage is dark brown across most of the upper side, with a black tail and a thin, curved white band at the uppertail coverts. The underside is mostly white with a brownish belly patch, dark underwing margins, and dark lines along the inner wing coverts. The head has a crisp, dark cap bordered by a nearly complete white collar. Great shearwaters fly with stiff wings, making high, arcing turns, and feed by diving from the air or from the water's surface. After breeding during our winter in south Atlantic islands, they disperse north, often forming large noisy groups at sea and following ships. The adult is illustrated.

Sooty Shearwater, *Puffinus griseus*
Family Procellariidae (Fulmars, Shearwaters)
Size: 17"
Season: Spring–fall
Habitat: Open ocean, sometimes near the coastline

The sooty shearwater is a relatively common seabird off the New England coast and can often be seen in huge flocks where food is abundant. It has relatively narrow wings; a long, thin, blackish bill; and dark feet. The plumage, true to its name, is a sooty gray brown overall except for a whitish patch along the greater coverts of the underside of the wings. Flight is a combination of rapid wing beats, glides, and arcing turns. Sooty shearwaters dive underwater for fish, squid, and invertebrates, propelled by their wings, and will readily follow fishing vessels at sea. The adult is illustrated.

Manx Shearwater,
Puffinus puffinus
Family Procellariidae (Fulmars, Shearwaters)
Size: 13.5"
Season: Spring–fall
Habitat: Open ocean

The Manx shearwater is a relatively small shearwater with entirely pelagic habits except at its breeding grounds (in the northeastern Atlantic) during summer. The body is streamlined, with narrow, pointed wings, a short tail, and a thin, dark bill with short, tube-nosed nostrils at the base (characteristic of this group). It is dark gray-brown above, white below, with a white crescent behind the dark auriculars, dark margins to the underwings, and white under-tail coverts. In the flying bird one can usually see the edges of the white sides at the rump. Flight is stiff and fast, and they often hold their wings straight out from their bodies, making arcing swoops just above the water's surface. Manx shearwaters form large groups, swimming on the surface or diving for food. The adult is illustrated.

Wilson's Storm-Petrel,
Oceanites oceanicus
Family Hydrobatidae (Storm-Petrels)
Size: 7"
Season: Spring–fall
Habitat: Coastal or offshore oceanic waters

The Wilson's storm-petrel is a small seabird that breeds in far southern islands and Antarctica, dispersing to the Northern Hemisphere during our summer. The wings are relatively short and rounded, the tail is square or slightly rounded, and long, thin legs extend beyond the tail. The head is large with a steep forehead and a stubby, tube-nosed bill. The plumage is grayish brown overall, except for a crisp, white rump patch that extends to the sides of the lower flanks, and pale edges to the inner coverts of the upper wings. Wilson's storm-petrels have purposeful flight with shallow wing beats, akin to a tern, dangle their feet, and skip along the water's surface while feeding. They gather in large groups at sea and commonly follow fishing vessels and whales. The adult is illustrated.

Leach's Storm-Petrel, *Oceanodroma leucorhoa*
Family Hydrobatidae (Storm-Petrels)
Size: 8"
Season: Summer
Habitat: Open ocean, offshore islands

Fairly common, the Leach's storm-petrel is a small, dark seabird with long, angled wings, a steep forehead, a forked tail, and a tube-nosed bill characteristic of this group. The plumage is dark brown to blackish, darkest on the tail and flight feathers, with a paler brown diagonal strip along the upper side of the inner wing. Populations in the Atlantic, including New England, have a white rump, while those in the southern Pacific have dark rumps. They come ashore only at night during breeding season and are mostly solitary at sea. Flight is varied but is often erratic and includes deep wing beats on bowed wings. Leach's storm-petrels patter across the water's surface on long, thin legs or hover to pick up small fish and other tiny prey. The adult is illustrated.

Northern Gannet, *Morus bassanus*

Family Sulidae (Gannets)
Size: 36"
Season: Year-round
Habitat: Open ocean close to shore, coastal cliffs

The name "gannet" derives from "gander" and alludes to the goose-like shape of this seabird. Often forming very large groups, the northern gannet alternates rapid wing beats with soaring flight. To feed, it forms its body into a sleek arrow shape and dramatically plunges headfirst into the ocean, completely submerging itself to catch fish. Its body is sleek and white with black flight feathers. The upper part of the head is pale yellow; the bill is thick, pointed, and bluish. The eye seems small and is enveloped in a thin black ring and lores. The juvenile is dark and spotted with white. The adult is illustrated.

American White Pelican,

Pelecanus erythrorhynchos
Family Pelecanidae (Pelicans)
Size: 62"
Season: Spring and fall transient
Habitat: Open freshwater, coastal areas

One of North America's largest birds, the American white pelican has a wingspan of over 9 feet. It is white overall with black flight feathers. The massive bill is orange and has a membranous, expandable throat pouch. In posture, it holds its neck in a characteristic strong kink and its folded wings in a peak along its back. American white pelicans often feed in cooperative groups, herding fish as they swim and scooping them up by dipping their bills in the water. They never plunge-dive like the brown pelican. When breeding, a strange horny growth appears on the upper mandible in both sexes. The nonbreeding adult is illustrated.

Brown Pelican,
Pelecanus occidentalis
Family Pelecanidae (Pelicans)
Size: 50"
Season: Summer
Habitat: Coastal waters

The majestic brown pelican enlivens coastal waters with its spectacular feeding process of plunge-diving for fish, headfirst, from some height. It often flies in formation inches from incoming swells, gaining lift and rarely needing to flap its wings. This pelican has a massive bill and bleached gray-brown plumage overall with a white head and neck. In breeding plumage the head is pale yellow with a brown-red nape patch and a black strip down the back of the neck. The brown pelican is quite gregarious and nests in trees or in slight depressions in the sand or rocks. The breeding adult is illustrated.

Double-crested Cormorant,
Phalacrocorax auritus
Family Phalacrocoracidae (Cormorants)
Size: 32"
Season: Summer
Habitat: Open freshwater or coastal areas

Named for the two long, white plumes that emerge from behind the eyes during breeding season, the double-crested cormorant is an expert swimmer that dives underwater to chase down fish. Because its plumage lacks the normal oils to repel water, it will stand with wings outstretched to dry itself. It is all black with a pale glossy cast on the back and wings. The eyes are bright green, the bill is thin and hooked, and the throat patch and lores are yellow. The breeding adult is illustrated.

Great Cormorant,
Phalacrocorax carbo
Family Phalacrocoracidae (Cormorants)
Size: 36"
Season: Year-round
Habitat: Coastlines, rocky coastal cliffs, islands

The great cormorant is the largest cormorant and is found throughout the world. It has a heavy body with a broad, angular head, thick neck, thick bill, short tail, and a yellow gular (throat) patch. The plumage is uniformly black with a blue or greenish gloss and has a white border behind the gular patch, stretching along the throat from eye to eye. During breeding season a white patch at the hip is evident, and thin, white plumes grow on the sides of the neck. The juvenile great cormorant has a white belly and a pale, brownish-gray neck. Gregarious both at and away from its breeding grounds on rocky cliffs, the great cormorant dives for fish, crustaceans, and mollusks. Typical of cormorants, they are often seen standing with their wings outstretched to dry them. The breeding adult is illustrated.

HERONS, EGRETS

American Bittern, *Botaurus lentiginosus*
Family Ardeidae (Herons, Egrets)
Size: 27"
Season: Summer
Habitat: Marshy areas with dense vegetation

The American bittern is a fairly large, secretive heron with a small head, a long, straight bill, and a thick body. It has a habit of standing still with its neck and bill pointed straight up to imitate the surrounding reeds. Its plumage is very cryptic: Above, it is variegated brown and tan, and below, it is pale brown or whitish with thick rust-colored streaking that extends up the neck. The bill is yellow green and dark on the upper mandible. A dark patch extends from the lower bill to the upper neck. The legs are yellow green and thick. American bitterns skulk slowly through reeds and grasses to catch frogs, insects, and invertebrates. The adult is illustrated.

Least Bittern, *Ixobrychus exilis*
Family Ardeidae (Herons, Egrets)
Size: 13"
Season: Summer
Habitat: Fresh or brackish marshes

The least bittern, the smallest heron, is secretive and more often heard than seen. It creeps and clambers through densely vegetated marshes searching for frogs, invertebrates, and other aquatic creatures, emitting a soft cooing call or kaw when disturbed. It is rarely seen in flight. Its back is a dark blue gray and its midwing and body a buffy brown with white streaking. The crown is dark gray, and the bill is yellow and pointed. Legs and feet are yellow with long, thin toes for grasping clumps of vegetation. The female is paler along the back and crown. When alarmed, it will stand motionless with its head straight up, imitating a stalk of reeds. The adult male is illustrated.

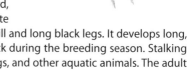

Great Egret, *Ardea alba*
Family Ardeidae (Herons, Egrets)
Size: 38"
Season: Summer
Habitat: Freshwater and saltwater marshes

A beautiful and stately bird, the great egret is all white with a long, thin yellow bill and long black legs. It develops long, lacy plumes across its back during the breeding season. Stalking slowly, it pursues fish, frogs, and other aquatic animals. The adult is illustrated.

Great Blue Heron, *Ardea herodias*
Family Ardeidae (Herons, Egrets)
Size: 46"
Season: Year-round
Habitat: Most aquatic areas, including lakes, creeks, and marshes

The great blue heron is the largest heron in North America. Walking slowly through shallow water or fields, it stalks fish, crabs, and small vertebrates, catching them with its massive bill. With long legs and a long neck, it is blue gray overall with a white face and a heavy yellow-orange bill. The crown is black and supports plumes of medium length. The front of the neck is white, with distinct black chevrons fading into breast plumes. In flight the neck is tucked back and the wing beats are regular and labored. The adult is illustrated.

Little Blue Heron, *Egretta caerulea*
Family Ardeidae (Herons, Egrets)
Size: 25"
Season: Summer
Habitat: Freshwater or coastal swamps

The little blue heron is a medium-size heron that skulks along shorelines with vegetative cover, often using its wings to cast a shadow over the water to see and attract fish. It is overall slate blue with a purple cast on the neck. The bill is pale gray with a dark tip, and the legs are greenish. The juvenile is all white with small, dark tips on the primaries, and it can be confused with other white herons. The adult is illustrated.

Tricolored Heron, *Egretta tricolor*
Family Ardeidae (Herons, Egrets)
Size: 26"
Season: Summer
Habitat: Salt marshes, mangrove swamps

The tricolored heron is a thin, bluish-gray heron with a white belly and brownish neck stripe and lower back. In nonbreeding plumage, it has yellow lores and an orangey bill, but in breeding season this area of the lores and bill are blue and the bill has a dark tip. It also develops plumes behind the ears and across the lower back. To feed, it will actively pursue prey or stand motionless, waiting to stab a fish or frog with its thin, spear-like bill. The breeding adult is illustrated.

Green Heron, *Butorides virescens*
Family Ardeidae (Herons, Egrets)
Size: 18"
Season: Summer
Habitat: Ponds, creeks, wetlands

The green heron is a compact, crow-size heron that perches on low branches over the water, crouching forward to search for fish, snails, and insects. It is known to toss a bug into the water to attract fish. The green heron is really not so green, but rather a dull grayish blue with a burgundy-chestnut-colored neck and black crown. The bill is dark, and the legs are bright yellow orange. When disturbed, its crest feathers will rise and it will stand erect and twitch its tail. It is fairly secretive and solitary. The adult is illustrated.

Snowy Egret, *Egretta thula*
Family Ardeidae (Herons, Egrets)
Size: 24"
Season: Summer
Habitat: Open water, marshes, swamps

The snowy egret is all white with lacy plumes across the back in breeding season. The bill is slim and black, and the legs are black with bright-yellow feet. The juvenile has greenish legs with a yellow stripe along the front. The snowy egret forages for fish and frogs along the shore by moving quickly, shuffling to stir up prey, which it then stabs with its bill. Sometimes it may run to pursue its prey. The name of this bird can be remembered by keeping in mind that it wears yellow "boots" because it is cold or "snowy." The breeding adult is illustrated.

Cattle Egret, *Bubulcus ibis*
Family Ardeidae (Herons, Egrets)
Size: 20"
Season: Summer
Habitat: Upland fields, often near cattle in grazing land

The cattle egret is a widespread species originally from Africa and now quite common throughout much of North America. Unlike most herons, it is not normally found in aquatic environments. It forms groups around cattle, often perching atop them, and feeds on insects aroused by the movement of their hooves. It is stocky and all white with a comparatively short yellow bill and short black legs. In breeding plumage the legs and bill turn a bright orange, and a peachy, pale yellow forms on the crown, breast, and back. The nonbreeding adult is illustrated.

Black-crowned Night-Heron,
Nycticorax nycticorax
Family Ardeidae (Herons, Egrets)
Size: 25"
Season: Summer
Habitat: Marshes, swamps with
wooded banks

The nocturnal black-crowned night-
heron is a stocky, thick-necked heron
with a comparatively large head and a sharp, heavy, thick bill. It
has pale-gray wings; white underparts; and a black crown, back,
and bill. The eyes are piercing red, the legs are yellow, and there
are white plumes on the rear of the head (longest during breeding). During the day it roosts in groups, but at night it forages
alone, waiting motionless for prey such as fish or crabs. It may
even raid the nests of other birds. Its voice is composed of low-
pitched barks and croaks. The adult is illustrated.

Yellow-crowned
Night-Heron, *Nyctanassa violacea*
Family Ardeidae (Herons, Egrets)
Size: 24"
Season: Summer
Habitat: Marshes, ponds, coastal shrubs

Shaped somewhat like the black-
crowned night-heron, the yellow-
crowned night-heron is blue gray
overall with a black face, white cheek patch, and slim, pale crown
that is not really yellow but whitish or pale buff. In breeding plumage it develops plumes from behind the crest. Its eyes are large
and red, and its legs are yellow. The immature bird is drab brown
gray, mottled with light streaks. It is nocturnal but will occasionally feed during the day for crustaceans and other aquatic animals, roosting in groups at night. The adult is illustrated.

Glossy Ibis, *Plegadis falcinellus*
Family Threskiornithidae (Ibises)
Size: 23"
Season: Summer
Habitat: Freshwater or brackish
marshes, bays, estuaries

The glossy ibis became estab-
lished in the United States only recently and is gradually expand-
ing its range. In appearance, it is like a small heron or a robust
curlew and is nearly identical to the white-faced ibis (which does
not occur in New England). It has long legs for wading, a short tail,
thin neck, and a long, stout, decurved bill for probing deep into
mud. The color is dark, chestnut brown overall, with darker, glossy,
greenish-brown wings, two thin whitish lines between the eye
and the bill, and dark eyes. Nonbreeding adults are darker overall
with a speckled brown-and-white head and neck. Unlike herons,
ibises fly with their necks outstretched, with quick wing beats
punctuated by short glides. They walk through shallow water and
mud, probing for a variety of prey including insects and crustaceans. The breeding adult is illustrated.

Black Vulture, *Coragyps atratus*
Family Cathartidae (New World Vultures)
Size: 25"
Season: Year-round
Habitat: Open, dry country

Like the turkey vulture, the black vulture is adept at soaring. Its
wing beats, however, are faster, and while soaring, it holds its
wings at a flat angle instead of a dihedral. It is stocky in physique
and has a short, stubby tail and shorter wings than the turkey
vulture. The primaries are pale on an otherwise black body, and
the head is bald and gray. It eats carrion and garbage and is quite
aggressive at feeding sites. The adult is illustrated.

Turkey Vulture, *Cathartes aura*
Family Cathartidae (New World Vultures)
Size: 27"
Season: Summer
Habitat: Open country

The turkey vulture is known for its effortless, skilled soaring. It will often soar for hours, without flapping, rocking in the breeze on 6-foot wings that form an upright V shape, or dihedral angle. It has a black body and inner wing, with pale flight feathers and tail feathers that give it a noticeable two-toned appearance from below. The tail is longish, and the feet extend no more than halfway past the base of the tail. The head is naked, red, and small, so the bird appears almost headless in flight. The bill is strongly hooked to aid in tearing apart its favored prey, carrion. The juvenile has a dark-gray head. Turkey vultures often roost in flocks and form groups around food or at a roadkill site. The adult is illustrated.

Osprey, *Pandion haliaetus*
Family Accipitridae (Kites, Hawks, Eagles)
Size: 23"; female larger than male
Season: Summer
Habitat: Always near water, salt or fresh

Also known as the fish hawk, the osprey exhibits a dramatic feeding method, plunging feetfirst into the water to snag fish. Sometimes it completely submerges itself, then laboriously flies off with its heavy catch. It is dark brown above and white below and has a distinct, dark eye stripe contiguous with the nape. Females often show a pale, mottled "necklace" across the breast, and juveniles have pale streaking on the back. The osprey flies with an obvious crook at the midwing, appearing gull-like, and its wings are long and narrow, with a dark carpal patch. The adult male is illustrated.

Mississippi Kite,
Ictinia mississippiensis
Family Accipitridae (Kites, Hawks, Eagles)
Size: 14"
Season: Summer
Habitat: Swamps, woodland edges, agricultural land

The Mississippi kite is North America's smallest kite, with a rounded head, short, hooked bill, and long wings and tail. Its plumage is slate gray across the back, undersides, and upperwing, with a paler head, becoming almost white. The tail and ends of the primaries are black, contrasting with the white secondaries. The lores and feathers surrounding the deep-red eyes are black. Sexes are similar, while juveniles show white spotting on the back and rufous spotting on the underside. In flight the wings are held flat and straight, and the outermost primary is noticeably shorter than the others. Mississippi kites feed in flight, snatching insects from the air or swooping low to attack small terrestrial animals. The voice is a high-pitched, relatively weak whistle in two parts. The adult is illustrated.

Golden Eagle, *Aquila chrysaetos*
Family Accipitridae (Kites, Hawks, Eagles)
Size: 30"; female larger than male
Season: Summer
Habitat: Mountainous areas, hills,
open country

The golden eagle is a solitary, very
large raptor resembling a buteo
(broad-winged, soaring hawk), with
large talons and long, broad wings
with a 6.5-foot wingspan. Its plumage is dark brown overall with
a pale-golden nape. It has a relatively small head with a bill that is
large and hooked, forming a wide gape. The juvenile shows a white
patch at the base of the tail and at the base of the flight feathers.
Golden eagles hold their wings horizontally or with a very slight
dihedral angle in flight. They forage from a perch or by soaring
overhead, attacking mammals, reptiles, and birds. They may also
eat carrion. The adult is illustrated.

Bald Eagle, *Haliaeetus leucocephalus*
Family Accipitridae (Kites, Hawks,
Eagles)
Size: 30"–40"; female larger than male
Season: Year-round
Habitat: Lakes, rivers with tall perches
or cliffs

The bald eagle is a large raptor that is widespread but fairly uncommon. It eats fish or scavenges dead animals and congregates in
large numbers where food is abundant. Its plumage is dark brown,
contrasting with its white head and tail. Juveniles show white
splotching across the wings and breast. The yellow bill is large and
powerful, and the talons are large and sharp. In flight its wings are
fairly flat and straight, resembling a long plank. Bald eagles make
huge nests of sticks high in trees. The adult is illustrated.

Sharp-shinned Hawk,
Accipiter striatus
Family Accipitridae (Kites, Hawks, Eagles)
Size: 10"–14"; female larger than male
Season: Year-round
Habitat: Woodlands, bushy areas

The sharp-shinned hawk is North America's smallest accipiter, with a longish, squared tail and stubby, rounded wings. Its short wings allow for agile flight in tight, wooded quarters, where it quickly attacks small birds in flight. Its upperparts are grayish, while below it is light and barred with pale-rufous stripes. The eyes are set forward on the face to aid in the direct pursuit of prey. The juvenile has white underparts streaked with brown. The sharp-shinned hawk may be confused with the larger Cooper's hawk, which has a more rounded tail. The adult is illustrated.

Cooper's Hawk, *Accipiter cooperii*
Family Accipitridae (Kites, Hawks, Eagles)
Size: 17", female larger than male
Season: Year-round
Habitat: Woodlands

The Cooper's hawk perches stealthily on branches in the canopy, then ambushes its prey of smaller birds or mammals by diving through the thickets. Its plumage is very similar to that of the sharp-shinned hawk, but the Cooper's hawk is larger in size and has a slightly longer rounded tail, thinner wings, and a relatively larger head. The eyes are set more in the middle of the face. Unlike the sharp-shinned hawk, the Cooper's hawk may perch and hunt in open country. The adult is illustrated.

Northern Goshawk, *Accipiter gentilis*
Family Accipitridae (Kites, Hawks, Eagles)
Size: 22"; female larger than male
Season: Year-round
Habitat: Mountains, forests

The northern goshawk is the largest accipiter, similar in shape to the Cooper's and sharp-shinned hawks but often mistaken for a buteo because of its large size. It is dark gray on the back and finely barred white and gray underneath. The head has a white superciliary stripe bordered by a dark crown and ear patch. Juveniles are mottled brown with coarse streaking across the breast and have more noticeably banded tails. Northern goshawks hunt from a perch, ambush-style, flying through woodlands to capture birds and mammals up to rabbit size. The adult is illustrated.

Northern Harrier, *Circus cyaneus*
Family Accipitridae (Kites, Hawks, Eagles)
Size: 18"; female larger than male
Season: Summer
Habitat: Open fields, wetlands

Also known as the marsh hawk, the northern harrier flies low to the ground, methodically surveying its hunting grounds for rodents and other small animals. When it spots prey, aided by its acute hearing, it will drop abruptly to the ground to attack. It is a thin raptor with long, flame-shaped wings that are broad in the middle and a long tail. The face has a distinct owl-like facial disk, and there is a conspicuous white patch at the rump. Males are gray above with a white-streaked breast and black wing tips. Females are brown with a barred breast. The juvenile is similar in plumage to the female but has a pale belly. The male (top) and female (bottom) are illustrated.

Red-shouldered Hawk, *Buteo lineatus*
Family Accipitridae (Kites, Hawks, Eagles)
Size: 17"
Season: Summer
Habitat: Wooded areas near water

The red-shouldered hawk is a solitary, small buteo with a long tail. It waits patiently on its perch before flying down to attack a variety of small animals. It has a banded black-and-white tail and spotted dark wings. The head and shoulder are rust colored, while the breast is light with rust barring. The legs are long and yellow, and the bill is hooked. In flight there is a pale arc just inside the wing tips, and it flaps its wings with quick beats followed by short glides. Western populations are darker overall than their eastern counterparts. The adult is illustrated.

Broad-winged Hawk,
Buteo platypterus
Family Accipitridae (Kites, Hawks, Eagles)
Size: 15"
Season: Summer
Habitat: Woodlands, roadsides

The broad-winged hawk is North America's smallest buteo. It summers in eastern North America and migrates in huge flocks to Central and South America in the winter. It is dark brown above, white below, with a reddish-brown breast that fades to spotting and barring across the belly and flanks. A rare dark morph is dark-brown overall. Both morphs have wide black-and-white bars across the tail, which are less developed in juvenile birds. In flight there is a dark border to the trailing edge of the otherwise light underwing, and the wings are held flat while soaring. Broad-winged hawks hunt for small mammals, reptiles, amphibians, or invertebrates often near a water source. Their voice is a piercing, very high-pitched *pe-seeee*. The adult light morph is illustrated.

Red-tailed Hawk, *Buteo jamaicensis*

Family Accipitridae (Kites, Hawks, Eagles)
Size: 20"
Season: Year-round
Habitat: Open country, prairies

This widespread species is the most common buteo in the United States. It has broad, rounded wings and a stout, hooked bill. Its plumage is highly variable depending on geographic location. In general, the underparts are light with darker streaking that forms a dark band across the belly. The upperparts are dark brown, and the tail is rufous. Light spotting occurs along the scapulars. In flight there is a noticeable dark patch along the inner leading edge of the underwing. Red-tailed hawks glide down from perches such as telephone poles and posts in open country to catch rodents, and they may also hover to spot prey. They are usually seen alone or in pairs. Their voice is the familiar *keeer!* The western adult is illustrated.

Rough-legged Hawk, *Buteo lagopus*

Family Accipitridae (Kites, Hawks, Eagles)
Size: 21"
Season: Winter
Habitat: Open country, areas near cliffs

The rough-legged hawk is a relatively long-winged and long-tailed buteo with a proportionately small bill and feet. Two color phases exist (light and dark), with the light phase being most common. It is mottled dark brown or grayish above and mixed creamy white and dark brown below, often with a concentration of dark at the belly, especially in females. In flight the central part of the wing is white, contrasting with darker coverts and tips of the flight feathers. The tail has a white base and a dark subterminal band. The legs are feathered for Arctic conditions (hence the common name). Rough-legged hawks search for small mammals or ground birds from a perch or while in flight, often hovering overhead. The light-phase adult is illustrated.

American Kestrel,
Falco sparverius
Family Falconidae (Falcons)
Size: 10"
Season: Year-round
Habitat: Open country, urban areas

North America's most common falcon, the American kestrel is a tiny, robin-size falcon with long, pointed wings and tail. Fast in flight, it hovers above fields or dives from its perch on branches or a wire to capture small animals and insects. The upperparts are rufous and barred with black, the wings are blue gray, and the breast is buff or white and streaked with black spots. The head is patterned with a gray crown and vertical patches of black on the face. The female has rufous wings and a barred tail. Also known as the sparrow hawk, it has a habit of flicking its tail up and down while perched. The adult male is illustrated.

Merlin, *Falco columbarius*
Family Falconidae (Falcons)
Size: 10"–12" (females larger than males)
Season: Year-round
Habitat: Open country, woodland edges, coastlines, farmland

The merlin is a pugnacious, stocky falcon, slightly larger and heavier than a kestrel, with pointed wings and a short, stubby bill. Three subspecies are recognized and vary by the degree of dark coloration. In general, the upperparts are some shade of gray (in males) or brown (in females) with variable amounts of light- to dark-brown streaking. Light individuals have only a faint moustachial patch, while dark individuals may have a mostly dark head. Merlins pursue small birds in direct, powerful flight or in sudden stoops. The adult male is illustrated.

FALCONS

Gyrfalcon, *Falco rusticolus*
Family Falconidae (Falcons)
Size: 22", female larger than male
Season: Winter
Habitat: Open country near cliffs

The gyrfalcon is a large, powerful falcon of the far north with a long tail and somewhat more-rounded wings than other falcons. Three color morphs exist—white, gray, and dark—with the gray being most common. It is slate gray above, heavily barred with white and gray below, and has dark facial markings across the eye and malar area. The white morph is snow white with dark-gray mottling on the back, tail, and wings. Gyrfalcons pursue birds and mammals up to duck and rabbit size in direct flight on stiff wings. The adult gray phase is illustrated.

Peregrine Falcon, *Falco peregrinus*
Family Falconidae (Falcons)
Size: 17"; female larger than male
Season: Summer
Habitat: Open country, cliffs, urban areas, coastal areas

The peregrine falcon is a powerful and agile raptor with long, sharply pointed wings. It is dark slate gray above and pale whitish below, with uniform barring below the breast. The head has a distinctive "helmet," with a white ear patch and chin contrasting with the blackish face and crown. Juveniles are mottled brown overall with heavy streaking on the underside. Peregrine falcons attack other birds in flight using spectacular high-speed aerial dives. Once threatened by DDT pollution that caused thinning of their eggshells, they have made a dramatic comeback. The adult is illustrated.

Yellow Rail, *Coturnicops noveboracensis*
Family Rallidae (Rails, Coots)
Size: 7"
Season: Summer
Habitat: Marshes, wetland areas with dense grasses and sedges

The yellow rail is a tiny rail, only slightly larger than the diminutive black rail, that is rarely seen due to its elusive and secretive habits. It seeks the shelter of dense vegetation, runs rather than flies when alarmed, and its voice, a series of *tic-tic-tic* notes, is often the only indication of its presence. The body is compact and plump with a short neck, short tail, and a stubby bill. The plumage is pale yellowish brown with alternating back and buff stripes, crossed with thick, white crescents along the back. On the head is a small, dark cap, a broad eye stripe, and a yellow or grayish bill. Juveniles show white speckles on the head and neck. In flight the white inner secondaries and underwing bases are revealed. The adult is illustrated.

Black Rail, *Laterallus jamaicensis*
Family Rallidae (Rails, Coots)
Size: 6"
Season: Summer
Habitat: Saltwater or freshwater wetlands

The black rail is a rare, diminutive, secretive rail that is difficult to see as it skulks in dense wetland vegetation. It is plump with a short tail and bill and has bright-red eyes. The plumage is dark gray brown above and slaty gray below, with white spotting across the back and flanks and a rust patch across the upper shoulders. Both sexes and juveniles are similar. Black rails are active mostly at night, voicing a ragged *kik-a dow,* or low cooing sound. They will often run rather than fly when disturbed. They forage among grasses for aquatic invertebrates, plants, and seeds. The adult is illustrated.

Virginia Rail, *Rallus limicola*
Family Rallidae (Rails, Coots)
Size: 9.5"
Season: Summer
Habitat: Freshwater or brackish marshes

The Virginia rail is a small, secretive, cryptic marsh bird with a proportionately long, reddish, downcurved bill. Its plumage is rusty brown overall with darker streaking on the back and black-and-white barring about the flanks. The head has a dark crown and lores and a gray face. The legs are thick, with long toes for support in the aquatic habitat. Virginia rails are active mostly at dawn and dusk, skulking through vegetation, probing the mud for worms, aquatic invertebrates, and plants. Their voice is a quick, repetitive, two- or three-part *kik-kik*. The adult is illustrated.

Sora, *Porzana carolina*
Family Rallidae (Rails, Coots)
Size: 9"
Season: Summer
Habitat: Marshes, meadows

The sora is a small, short-tailed, chicken-shaped rail with long, thin toes. Its plumage is mottled rusty brown above and grayish below with white barring along the belly and sides. The head has a black patch between the eye and bill, and the bill is yellow and conical. The tail is pointed and often cocked up and flicked. The juvenile is pale brown below, with less black on the face. Soras feed along shorelines or at the edges of meadows for snails, insects, and aquatic plants. Their voice is a soft, rising *ooo-EEP,* and they are quite tame, being seen more often than other rails. The breeding adult is illustrated.

Clapper Rail, *Rallus longirostris*
Family Rallidae (Rails, Coots)
Size: 14"
Season: Summer
Habitat: Coastal saltwater or brackish marshes

Also known as the marsh hen, the clapper rail is very shy and difficult to see. It lurks through marshy vegetation and usually chooses to walk or swim rather than fly. It forages by probing through mud and grass for a variety of small prey, vocalizing harsh, clattering *kek-kek-kek* sounds in rapid succession. It is a relatively thin rail with a long, slightly decurved bill. The plumage is gray brown above with a pale rust breast and barred flanks. The adult is illustrated.

King Rail, *Rallus elegans*
Family Rallidae (Rails, Coots)
Size: 15"
Season: Summer
Habitat: Freshwater marshes, fields, occasionally brackish wetlands

Endangered in some regions, the king rail is a large, secretive rail of primarily freshwater habitats. The very similar clapper rail is found mostly in brackish areas. It is shaped just like the clapper rail with a long, stout bill, short tail and wings, and a thin, chicken-like body. The coloration is similar too, but the king has bolder, black barring on the lower flanks, and an orange-brown cast overall (not grayish). King rails skulk through tall grasses, sedges, or cattails, searching for a wide variety of prey including insects, crustaceans, fish, and plants. Its voice is a series of sharp, raspy, metallic *kek* notes or a singe note followed by a trill. The adult is illustrated.

American Coot,
Fulica americana
Family Rallidae (Rails, Coots)
Size: 15"
Season: Year-round
Habitat: Wetlands, ponds,
urban lawns and parks

The American coot has a plump body and a thick head and neck. A relatively tame bird, it is commonly seen in urban areas and parks. It dives for fish to feed, but it will also dabble like a duck or pick food from the ground. It is dark gray overall with a black head and white bill that ends with a dark, narrow ring. The white trailing edge of the wings can been seen in flight. The toes are flanked with lobes that enable the coot to walk on water plants and swim efficiently. Juveniles are similar in plumage to adults but paler. Coots are often seen in very large flocks. The adult is illustrated.

Common Moorhen,
Gallinula chloropus
Family Rallidae (Rails, Coots)
Size: 14"
Season: Summer
Habitat: Freshwater ponds and
wetlands

The common moorhen, like the coot, is actually a type of rail that behaves more like a duck. It paddles along, bobbing its head up and down, picking at the water surface for any small aquatic animals, insects, or plants. Having short wings, it is a poor flier, but its very long toes allow it to walk on floating vegetation. It is overall dark gray with a brownish back, black head, and white areas on the tail and sides. In breeding plumage the forehead shield is deep red and the bill is red with a yellow tip. Also known as the common gallinule. The breeding adult is illustrated.

Black-bellied Plover, *Pluvialis squatarola*
Family Charadriidae (Plovers)
Size: 11"
Season: Winter
Habitat: Open areas, coastal or inland

The black-bellied plover is a relatively large plover with long, pointed wings and a whistling flight call. Like other plovers, it feeds by scooting quickly along the ground, stopping suddenly to peck at small prey in the mud or sand, and then scooting along again. Its winter plumage is gray above and paler below, with a white belly. The bill is black, short, and thick. A distinctive black patch on the axillary feathers can be seen in flight. In breeding plumage it develops the sharply contrasting black belly, face, and front of neck. The nonbreeding adult (top) and breeding adult (bottom) are illustrated.

American Golden-Plover, *Pluvialis dominica*
Family Charadriidae (Plovers)
Size: 10.5"
Season: Spring and fall migrant
Habitat: Open fields, pastures

The American golden-plover was previously considered con-specific (of the same species) with the Pacific golden plover, as the lesser golden plover. It is similar to the black-bellied plover but slightly smaller with a smaller bill and darker tail region. The breeding male is mottled golden brown and black above, black below and on the face and throat, and white above the eye and down the sides of the neck. The crown is dark. Nonbreeding adults are mottled gray and brown with a pale supercilium below a contrasting dark crown. They eat a variety of insects, larvae, and plant matter, gleaned by scooting about and pecking at the ground. The nonbreeding adult (top) and breeding adult (bottom) are illustrated.

Semipalmated Plover,
Charadrius semipalmatus
Family Charadriidae (Plovers)
Size: 7"
Season: Spring and fall migrant
Habitat: Open sand or mudflats,
coastal beaches

The semipalmated plover is a small, plump plover with pointed wings, large black eyes, and a relatively large, rounded head. It has a dark-brown back and crown, is white below, and has a small, orange bill with a dark tip. The head has dark bands across the eyes and encircling the neck. The legs and feet are yellow. Winter and breeding plumages are similar, with the exception of an all-dark bill and a lighter supercilium in winter. This widespread plover flies in flocks but disperses to feed, when it uses fast running interrupted by sudden stops to probe for invertebrates. The plover's name is derived from the partial webbing at the base of its toes. The breeding adult (bottom) and winter/nonbreeding adult (top) are illustrated.

Killdeer, *Charadrius vociferus*
Family Charadriidae (Plovers)
Size: 10"
Season: Summer
Habitat: Inland fields, farmlands,
lakeshores, meadows

The killdeer gets its name from its piercing *kill-dee* call, which is often heard before these well-camouflaged plovers are seen. Well adapted to human-altered environments, it is quite widespread and gregarious. It has long, pointed wings, a long tail, and a conspicuous double-banded breast. The upperparts are dark brown, the belly is white, and the head is patterned with a white supercilium and forehead. The tail is rusty orange with a black tip. In flight there is a noticeable white stripe across the flight feathers. The killdeer is known for the classic "broken wing" display that it uses to distract predators from its nest and young. The adult is illustrated.

Piping Plover, *Charadrius melodus*
Family Charadriidae (Plovers)
Size: 7"
Season: Summer
Habitat: Open sand or mudflats, coastal beaches

The piping plover is rare and threatened due to disturbance to its open, sandy habitat and is often heard before being seen because of its cryptic coloration. It is a small plover with a short, thick bill. Its plumage is pale sandy gray above and white below with a gray breast band. The legs are orange. In breeding plumage the breast band is black, there is a black patch above the forehead, and the bill turns orange with a black tip. Juveniles are similar to winter adults. In flight the white tail coverts and wing bars are conspicuous. Piping plovers scoot and stop across the sand, pecking for small invertebrates, and voice a sharp, high-pitched *pip-pip-pip* or *pee-low*. The breeding adult (bottom) and nonbreeding adult (top) are illustrated.

American Oystercatcher,
Haematopus palliatus
Family Haematopodidae (Oystercatchers)
Size: 18"
Season: Summer
Habitat: Coastal beaches, tide pools

The American oystercatcher is a chunky, short-tailed, and short-winged shorebird with a dark-brown back, white belly, and black head. It has a heavy, knifelike, bright-red bill, yellow eyes, and stocky, salmon-colored legs. In flight there is a distinct white bar across the secondary feathers. It follows the tidal pattern, foraging at low tide and roosting at high tide in groups with other shorebirds and gulls. It uses its bill to pry away shellfish—including oysters—from rocks, or to probe for worms. The bill is also used to jam open bivalves and devour the flesh. Its voice is a loud, piping call. The adult is illustrated.

American Avocet,

Recurvirostra americana
Family Recurvirostridae (Avocets, Stilts)
Size: 18"
Season: Spring and fall migrant
Habitat: Shallow wetlands, marshes

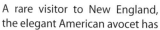

A rare visitor to New England,
the elegant American avocet has

a long, delicate, upturned black bill and long, thin, blue-gray legs. The upperparts are patterned black and white, the belly is white, and the head and neck are a light orange brown, which contrasts sharply with the bird's black eyes The bill of the female is slightly shorter than that of the male and has a greater bend. Nonbreeding adults have a pale-gray head and neck. Avocets use a side-to-side sweeping motion of the bill to stir up small crustaceans and insect larvae as they wade methodically through the shallows. They may even submerge their heads as the water deepens. They are adept swimmers and emit a *wheet!* call in alarm. The breeding female (top) and breeding male (bottom) are illustrated.

SANDPIPERS, PHALAROPES

Willet, *Catoptrophorus semipalmatus*

Family Scolopacidae (Sandpipers, Phalaropes)
Size: 15"
Season: Summer
Habitat: Saltwater and freshwater wetlands, coastal beaches

The willet is a heavy shorebird with a stout bill and conspicuous black-and-white wing markings in flight. Plumage is overall mocha brown above and pale below with extensive mottling in the breeding season. It has white lores and eye rings, and its plain gray legs are thick and sturdy. Found singly or in scattered flocks, it feeds by picking or probing for crabs, crustaceans, and worms in the mud and sand. Its call is a loud *wil-let,* often uttered in flight. The summer breeding adult is illustrated.

Spotted Sandpiper,
Actitis macularius
Family Scolopacidae (Sandpipers, Phalaropes)
Size: 7.5"
Season: Summer
Habitat: Streamsides, edges of lakes and ponds, coastal areas

The spotted sandpiper is known for its exaggerated, constant bobbing motion. It has a compact body, long tail, and short neck, wings, and legs. Its plumage is brown above and light below with a white shoulder patch. There is a white eye ring and superciliary stripe above the dark eye line. In breeding plumage it develops heavy spotting from the chin to lower flanks and barring on the back. The bill is orange with a dark tip. In flight the upper wings show a thin white stripe. To forage, it teeters about, picking small water prey and insects from the shoreline. The breeding adult is illustrated.

Greater Yellowlegs,
Tringa melanoleuca
Family Scolopacidae (Sandpipers, Phalaropes)
Size: 14"
Season: Spring and fall migrant
Habitat: Inland marshes, coastal areas

The greater yellowlegs, sometimes called the "telltale" bird, can act as a sentinel of a flock by raising an alarm when danger is near, flying off and circling to return. It has long, bright-yellow legs; a long neck; a dark, slightly upturned bill; and a white eye ring. The upperparts are dark gray and mottled, while the underparts are white with barring on the flanks. In breeding plumage the barring is noticeably darker and more extensive. To feed, it strides forward actively to pick small aquatic prey from the water or chase fish. The lesser yellowlegs is similar but smaller. The nonbreeding adult is illustrated.

Upland Sandpiper, *Bartramia longicauda*
Family Scolopacidae (Sandpipers, Phalaropes)
Size: 11.5"
Season: Summer
Habitat: Open fields, meadows

The upland sandpiper is closely related to the curlews, yet in many ways resembles a tall plover. It has a small head, large black eyes, a very thin neck, long tail, and long, yellowish legs. The bill is straight and relatively short and is yellow with a black tip. The plumage (similar in all seasons) is mottled and streaked with light and dark browns above and white below, with dark barring on the flanks. Solitary in nature, the upland sandpiper forages for insects and seeds among grasses, and often perches on raised rocks or posts. It curiously keeps its wings raised for a few moments after landing. Its voice includes a slow, strange, ascending and descending throaty whistle. The adult is illustrated.

Whimbrel, *Numenius phaeopus*
Family Scolopacidae (Sandpipers, Phalaropes)
Size: 17"
Season: Spring and fall migrant
Habitat: Coastal flats, inland marshes

Also known as the Hudsonian curlew, the whimbrel is a large shore-bird with a very long, decurved bill. It is overall gray brown, and paler beneath with barring. The head has a dark eye stripe and cap, with a pale central crown-stripe, and the legs are dark gray. The plumages in all seasons are similar. The whimbrel forages singly or in small groups, probing or picking with its long, sensitive bill, searching for invertebrates and coaxing fiddler crabs from their burrows. Their call is a soft *ker-loo*. The adult is illustrated.

Hudsonian Godwit,
Limosa haemastica
Family Scolopacidae (Sandpipers, Phalaropes)
Size: 15.5"
Season: Fall migrant
Habitat: Coastal shorelines, mudflats, freshwater wetlands

The Hudsonian godwit occasionally passes through New England on its lengthy migration from its breeding grounds in Alaska and northern Canada to its winter habitat in South America. It is a relatively large, gangly shorebird (although the smallest of the godwits) with long legs and a long, thin, slightly upturned bill. Breeding adults are dark overall, with deep, reddish-brown underparts, a mottled black, brown, and white back, pale neck, and a dark eye stripe. The bill is pinkish or orangey with a black tip. In flight the black underwing lining, white upperwing stripe, and white rump are evident. Non-breeding adults are unmarked gray overall. They wade in the water as high as their bellies and probe deep into mud or sand in search of invertebrate prey. The breeding adult is illustrated.

Marbled Godwit, *Limosa fedoa*
Family Scolopacidae (Sandpipers, Phalaropes)
Size: 18"
Season: Spring and fall migrant
Habitat: Coastal beaches, mudflats, inland fields

As its name suggests, the marbled godwit is marbled, or barred, with dark across its buff body, although the underside lacks marbling in winter plumage. The long pinkish bill has a slight upcurved portion at the tip, where it becomes dark in color. The legs are dark, and the underwing is a rich cinnamon color. It also has a light superciliary stripe above a dark eye line. Marbled godwits move about with slow, steady progress and probe in shallow water to find aquatic worms and crustaceans. Their call is a loud *god-WIT*. The adult is illustrated.

Ruddy Turnstone,
Arenaria interpres
Family Scolopacidae (Sandpipers, Phalaropes)
Size: 9.5"
Season: Winter
Habitat: Wide variety of shoreline habitats, from rocky intertidal sites to beaches and mudflats

The gregarious, frenetic ruddy turnstone is a chunky, short-legged shorebird with a short, wedge-shaped bill. The breeding adult has ruddy and black upperparts, a white belly, and a complex pattern of black and white on the head. The nonbreeding bird is pale brown and black above, with drab head markings. The stubby legs are orange. In flight the bird is white below and strongly patterned light and dark above. Turnstones bustle about constantly to pick, pry, or probe for almost any food item. Indeed, it will "turn stones" to search for its prey. The nonbreeding adult (top) and breeding adult (bottom) are illustrated.

Red Knot, *Calidris canutus*
Family Scolopacidae (Sandpipers, Phalaropes)
Size: 10.5"
Season: Winter
Habitat: Coastal beaches and mudflats

The red knot is a compact, short-legged shorebird with a slightly downcurved bill. In nonbreeding plumage it is mottled gray-brown above and pale below with light streaking. In breeding plumage it has a rufous body with a grayish back and wings. The bill is dark, about the length of the head. In flight the long, pointed wings, which are gray underneath, can be seen. It forages by probing and picking in the mud or sand for a variety of small prey. It often forms tight flocks while roosting and feeding. The breeding adult (bottom) and a nonbreeding adult (top) is illustrated.

Sanderling, *Calidris alba*
Family Scolopacidae (Sandpipers, Phalaropes)
Size: 8"
Season: Winter
Habitat: Coastal beaches, mudflats

The sanderling is a common shorebird that runs back and forth following the incoming and outgoing surf, grabbing small invertebrates exposed by the waves. It is a small, active, squat sandpiper with a short bill and legs. Its nonbreeding plumage is very pale above and white below, while the legs and bill are a contrasting black. There is a distinct black shoulder and leading edge of the wing. Females in breeding plumage are speckled brown above, while males develop rufous tones on the back, head, and neck. In flight a white stripe on the upper wing is visible. Sanderlings may form large foraging flocks and even larger flocks while roosting. The nonbreeding adult is illustrated.

Semipalmated Sandpiper, *Calidris pusilla*

Family Scolopacidae (Sandpipers, Phalaropes)
Size: 6"
Season: Spring and fall migrant
Habitat: Coastal beaches, mudflats

The semipalmated sandpiper is similar to the slightly larger western sandpiper, but it is present only during spring and fall migrations between breeding regions in northern Canada and Alaska and wintering grounds in South America. One of the "peeps," or very small sandpipers, it is a plump little shorebird with dark legs and a thin, straight bill (unlike the slightly drooping bill of the western sandpiper). Breeding plumage is mottled brownish and black above and white below, with limited dark streaking on the breast. Evident in flight are the white underwings, dark upperwings with a thin, white stripe, and a dark central stripe on the otherwise white tail. Winter plumage is grayer overall on the upperparts, head, and breast. This species is named because of the slight webbing between the toes, but this is difficult to discern in the field. They typically form large flocks as they scurry along the sand and mud, pecking for aquatic invertebrates. The breeding (bottom) and nonbreeding (top) adults are illustrated.

Western Sandpiper, *Calidris mauri*

Family Scolopacidae (Sandpipers, Phalaropes)
Size: 6.5"
Season: Spring and fall migrant
Habitat: Saltwater and freshwater wetlands, mudflats, coastal beaches

The western sandpiper is another one of the "peeps," or very small sandpipers, and nearly identical to the semipalmated sandpiper. It has a relatively long black bill that droops slightly and black legs. In winter it is pale gray brown above and white below. In breeding plumage the scapulars and face are rufous, and the breast and back show much-darker streaking. A thin white stripe on the upper wing is visible in flight, along with a white rump with a dark central stripe. Western sandpipers feed in shallow water or at the tide line, probing for invertebrates and insects. They often form rather large flocks. The nonbreeding adult (top) and breeding adult (bottom) are illustrated.

Least Sandpiper, *Calidris minutilla*

Family Scolopacidae (Sandpipers, Phalaropes)
Size: 6"
Season: Spring and fall migrant
Habitat: Coastal or freshwater marshes, mudflats

The least sandpiper is the smallest of the small sandpipers known as peeps. It has a thin, dark bill that droops slightly at the tip and has pale-yellowish legs (other peeps are dark legged). In breeding plumage the upperparts are brownish with dark-brown mottling. The underparts are white with a heavily streaked, brownish breast. Winter adults are similar but take on a grayish cast (but still retain some brown). Least sandpipers walk across wet ground, bending forward to pick for food, and voice a one- or two-part high-pitched *peep*. The breeding adult is illustrated.

Pectoral Sandpiper, *Calidris melanotos*
Family Scolopacidae (Sandpipers, Phalaropes)
Size: 9"
Season: Spring and fall migrant
Habitat: Mudflats, grassy wetlands, marshes, shorelines

The pectoral sandpiper visits New England en route to and from breeding grounds in Alaska and northern Canada and winter grounds in South America, avoiding submerged areas in favor of exposed, weedy fields and mudflats. It is medium size with a deep chest, small head, longish neck, yellow legs, and a narrow, medium-length, straight bill that droops slightly at the tip. Breeding plumage is streaked brown, black, and tan above and on the head and neck, with dense streaking on the breast meeting abruptly with a clean, white belly. In flight a very thin wing stripe and dark central tail feathers are evident. Winter plumage is similar but paler and grayer overall. Pectoral sandpipers pick food from the surface such as insects, aquatic invertebrates, and crustaceans, and usually run to the shelter of grasses rather than fly away when alarmed. The breeding adult is illustrated.

Purple Sandpiper, *Calidris maritima*
Family Scolopacidae (Sandpipers, Phalaropes)
Size: 9"
Season: Winter
Habitat: Rocky coastline and intertidal zones

The purple sandpiper breeds in the Canadian Arctic (farther north than any other shorebird) and winters along most of the north and mid-Atlantic coast. Its body is quite plump, with a large, roundish head, medium-length, thin, slightly drooping bill, and short legs. In breeding plumage the upperparts are heavily streaked in brown, gray, and black, the belly is white, and the legs and bill base are orangey. In New England it is most commonly seen in its winter plumage, which is nearly uniform gray above and white below, with sparse streaking on the flanks and breast. The legs and bill base also take on a brighter yellow-orange hue. The name is derived from a subtle purple sheen sometimes seen on the back of winter adults. Purple sandpipers scramble among algae-covered rocks for insects and marine invertebrates, and voice a sporadic, single, squeaking note, sometimes combined in an extended trill. The nonbreeding adult is illustrated.

Dunlin, *Calidris alpina*
Family Scolopacidae (Sandpipers, Phalaropes)
Size: 8.5"
Season: Fall–spring
Habitat: Coastal beaches, mudflats

This bird's name comes from the word "dun," a dull, gray-brown color, which aptly describes the winter plumage of the dunlin. It is a rather small sandpiper with a long bill that droops down at the tip. In breeding plumage there is a black belly patch and rufous tones on the back. In flight a white stripe on the upper wing and a white rump separated by a central dark line can be seen. It forms huge flocks, swirling and circling in unison. The dunlin walks steadily through shallow waters to feed, probing for crustaceans and other invertebrates. The nonbreeding adult (top) and breeding adult (bottom) are illustrated.

Long-billed Dowitcher,
Limnodromus scolopaceus
Family Scolopacidae (Sandpipers, Phalaropes)
Size: 11.5"
Season: Spring–fall
Habitat: Shorelines, mudflats, grassy wetlands

The long-billed dowitcher is a chunky shorebird with a long, straight, dark-gray bill. Breeding adults are mottled reddish-brown, black, and white above, with a blackish tail thinly barred with buff. The underparts are rufous with barring along the flanks and upper breast and streaking along the neck. The legs are dull yellow. Nonbreeding adults are grayish overall except for a white belly and supercilium. The similar short-billed dowitcher is a bit smaller and has only a marginally shorter bill. The dowitcher feeds by jerking its head up and down (like a sewing machine) in mudflats, probing for crustaceans and insects. Its voice is a fast-paced chatter or single, high *keek* notes. The breeding adult is illustrated.

Wilson's Snipe, *Gallinago delicata*
Family Scolopacidae (Sandpipers, Phalaropes)
Size: 10.5"
Season: Summer
Habitat: Saltwater and freshwater marshes

Also known as the common snipe, the Wilson's snipe is a cryptically marked, short-necked shorebird with a long, straight bill. The head is striped, and the back is flanked with white stripes bordering the scapulars. The underside is white, with extensive black barring, and the legs are short and pale greenish yellow. Plumage is similar in all seasons. While feeding, snipes probe rhythmically and deeply into the muddy substrate to extract worms, insect larvae, and crustaceans. It voices a loud *skipe!* when alarmed, or a *whit-whit-whit-whit*. Secretive and solitary, it will abruptly lift into flight when alarmed. Its flight is erratic and zigzagging and includes displays of "winnowing," where air across the tail feathers whistles during a steep descent. The adult is illustrated.

American Woodcock, *Scolopax minor*
Family Scolopacidae (Sandpipers, Phalaropes)
Size: 11"
Season: Summer
Habitat: Woodland edges with brush; moist fields

The American woodcock is a reclusive shorebird of upland woods and fields with a plump body, large head, long bill, stubby tail, and short legs. Its plumage is mottled gray above with distinct, paler-gray stripes down the sides of the back and is plain buff to pale orange underneath. The head contains two large, black eyes set high up on the face, and has a dark crown with transverse buff stripes. Woodcocks are mostly active at night or dusk, probing soft soils for earthworms and insects. They voice a blunt, nasal sound and produce a whistling noise in flight from air passing through their thin, outer primary feathers. The adult is illustrated.

Wilson's Phalarope, *Phalaropus tricolor*
Family Scolopacidae (Sandpipers, Phalaropes)
Size: 9"
Season: Summer
Habitat: Shallow pools around grassy or muddy wetlands

The Wilson's phalarope is a thin, elegant, small shorebird with a relatively long neck and a long, needlelike black bill. Among phalaropes, the female is the more brightly colored sex. In breeding plumage the female has a gray-brown back, clean white underparts, and a pale orange-brown throat. A thin black stripe runs from the bill, across the eye, and down the neck to the back. The head has pale cheeks and a gray crown, and the legs are black. Winter plumage is pale gray above and white below, and the legs are yellow. The breeding male looks like the winter adult female, with a dark eye stripe, crown, and nape. Wilson's phalaropes actively walk along shorelines or swim in circles to find insects or plant material. The breeding male (top) and breeding female (bottom) are illustrated.

Red-necked Phalarope,
Phalaropus lobatus
Family Scolopacidae (Sandpipers, Phalaropes)
Size: 7.5"
Season: Spring–fall migrant
Habitat: Offshore waters

The red-necked phalarope is the smallest phalarope; a dainty shorebird with short legs and a dark, needle-thin bill. As in all phalaropes, the female is the more colorful sex. In breeding plumage it is slate gray above with pale-orange streaks on the scapulars and is white below with a gray breast. The throat is white, and there is a distinctive U-shaped rufous patch on the sides of the neck. The breeding male is similar but duller overall. Nonbreeding adults are gray above and white below with a black post-ocular patch. Phalaropes feed on bits of food at the water's surface, sometimes swimming in tight circles to agitate the water. The nonbreeding adult (top) and breeding female (bottom) are illustrated.

Red Phalarope,
Phalaropus fulicarius
Family Scolopacidae (Sandpipers, Phalaropes)
Size: 8"
Season: Fall migrant
Habitat: Open ocean

The red phalarope is a stocky phalarope with a relatively thick neck and a thick, yellow bill. The female is the more brightly colored sex. While breeding, its plumage is deep rufous below and about the neck, with a streaked black-and-tan back and scapulars. The head is black with a bold white face. Breeding males are similar but paler overall. Nonbreeding adults are gray above, white below, and have a dark patch behind the eyes. Visible in flight, the underwing is white, and the upperwing is darker with a white wing stripe. In typical phalarope fashion, it feeds by picking insects or small aquatic prey from the water's surface, often twirling in circles. The breeding female is illustrated.

Ivory Gull, *Pagophila eburnea*
Family Laridae (Gulls, Terns)
Size: 18"
Season: Winter
Habitat: Open marine waters

A true bird of the Arctic, the ivory gull breeds and stays through winter in the coldest, northernmost regions of North America, occasionally dipping south to the New England coast. It is a stocky, short-legged gull with a large, rounded head and small, darkish bill with a yellow tip. Plumage is pure white overall, contrasting only with the black eyes and legs. Juvenile birds show black smudging on the front of the face and black spotting on the wings. It is an opportunistic feeder, foraging for a variety of food including fish, marine invertebrates, and carrion. The adult is illustrated.

Bonaparte's Gull, *Chroicocephalus philadelphia*
Family Laridae (Gulls, Terns)
Size: 13"
Season: Fall–spring
Habitat: Coastal in winter, most inland areas
during migration

The Bonaparte's gull is a small gull named after an American ornithologist who was related to Napoleon. It is agile and tern-like in flight, skimming low over the water to snatch fish. It has a thin, sharp black bill and red legs. Plumage in breeding season includes a black head that contrasts with its white body and light gray back and wings. The primaries form a white triangle against the dark trailing edge when in flight. The nonbreeding adult has a mostly white head with black eyes and small dark spots around the ears. A solitary gull, it does not form large flocks. Bonaparte's gulls build nests made of sticks in evergreen trees. The nonbreeding adult (top) and breeding adult (bottom) are illustrated.

Black-headed Gull,

Chroicocephalus ridibundus
Family Laridae (Gulls, Terns)
Size: 16"
Season: Winter
Habitat: Coastal estuaries, parks,
agricultural fields, lakes

The black-headed gull is a medium-size, dark-headed gull that is common in Europe and western Asia but makes only rare appearances in New England and Newfoundland. It looks much like a larger version of the Bonaparte's gull, with its pale-gray upperparts, white underparts, white leading edge to the primaries and black trailing edge, and dark head (in breeding plumage). However, the hood is dark brown (not black) and only covers the front half of the head. Also, the thin bill and legs are dark red. Winter adults have no dark hood but gray smudged behind and above the eyes. Gregarious and vocal, black-headed gulls are opportunistic feeders, eating a variety of terrestrial or aquatic invertebrates, plant matter, or carrion. The breeding adult (bottom) and nonbreeding adult (top) are illustrated.

Little Gull, *Hydrocoloeus minutus*
Family Laridae (Gulls, Terns)
Size: 11"
Season: Winter
Habitat: Coastal shores, estuaries, bays, lakes

The aptly named little gull is the smallest gull, with a stocky body, short legs, rounded wings, domed head, and a delicate, thin bill. It has a pale-gray mantle and white underparts, the upper wings are pale gray with a white trailing edge (no black on the wingtips), and the underwings are dark gray, also with a white trailing edge. In breeding plumage the head has a full, black hood, while in winter the head is white with a dark ear patch and smudging on the crown. The legs are red and the bill is blackish or dark red. Their behavior and posture are reminiscent of a tern, with erratic, buoyant flight on fast wing beats. They hunt for insects in the air or dabble at the water's surface and voice a series of short, repeated, nasal *kek* notes. The breeding adult (bottom) and nonbreeding adult (top) are illustrated.

GULLS, TERNS

Laughing Gull, *Leucophaeus atricilla*
Family Laridae (Gulls, Terns)
Size: 16"
Season: Summer
Habitat: Coastal beaches and marshes, urban environments, pastures

The laughing gull is so named because of its loud, often incessant laughing squawk. Social and uninhibited, it is a relatively thin, medium-size gull with long, pointed wings. The breeding adult has a black head with white eye arcs and a dark-red bill. Upperparts are dark gray, underparts are white, and wing tips are black with small white dots at the ends. The nonbreeding adult has a white head with faint dark smudging behind the eye. Laughing gulls eat crabs, fish, and worms and will scavenge from humans for food or even steal from other birds. The breeding adult (bottom) and a nonbreeding adult (top) are illustrated.

Ring-billed Gull,
Larus delawarensis
Family Laridae (Gulls, Terns)
Size: 18"
Season: Year-round
Habitat: Widespread from coast to inland lakes, ponds, parking lots

The ring-billed gull is common and quite tame. It is a relatively small gull with a rounded white head and a yellow bill with a dark subterminal ring. It has white underparts and a pale-gray back with black primaries tipped with white. The eyes are pale yellow, and the legs are yellow. The nonbreeding adult has faint streaking on the nape and around the eyes. Ring-billed gulls feed on the water or on the ground, taking a wide variety of food, and may scavenge in urban areas and dumps. The nonbreeding adult is illustrated.

Herring Gull, *Larus argentatus*
Family Laridae (Gulls, Terns)
Size: 25"
Season: Year-round
Habitat: Wetlands, coastal beaches, fields

The widespread herring gull occurs across the North American continent. It is a large, relatively thin, white-headed gull with a pale-gray back and white underparts. The bill is thick and yellow, with a reddish spot at the tip of the lower mandible. The primaries are black with white-spotted tips. The nonbreeding adult has brown streaking across the nape and neck. The legs are pink, and the eyes are pale yellow to ivory colored. Herring gulls are opportunistic feeders, eating fish, worms, crumbs, and trash. They are known to drop shellfish from the air to crack open their shells. The nonbreeding adult (top) and breeding adult (bottom) are illustrated.

Thayer's Gull, *Larus thayeri*
Family Laridae (Gulls, Terns)
Size: 23"
Season: Winter
Habitat: Coastal areas, harbors, fields; inland along watercourses

Once considered a subspecies of the herring gull and now considered most closely related to darker versions of the Iceland gull, the Thayer's gull can be difficult to distinguish in the field. It is a large, stocky gull with pink feet, a yellow bill with a red spot near the tip of the lower mandible, and dark eyes (some individuals will show light-yellow eyes). Its plumage is a fairly pale slate gray above, white below, with black markings on the outer primaries. While wintering, the head and neck are streaked brownish. Subadult gulls are variously mottled in browns and grays, with all-dark or dark-tipped bills. Thayer's gulls, which pick food from the ground or water, have a highly varied diet. The adult is illustrated.

Iceland Gull, *Larus glaucoides*
Family Laridae (Gulls, Terns)
Size: 22"
Season: Winter
Habitat: Coastal areas, bays, inlets; rarely inland

The Iceland gull is a hardy, medium-size gull that breeds in the Arctic and visits New England and eastern Canada in the winter. It is quite similar to the Thayer's gull, and even considered by some to be the same species, but Thayer's is most commonly found on the Pacific coast. It is stocky with a rounded crown, a medium-length yellow bill with a red spot on the lower mandible, and pinkish legs. The plumage is white with a pale-gray mantle and upper wings, solid white underwings, and some dark gray on the primary tips (some individuals have no gray at all, with a completely white trailing edge to the wing). Winter adults have variable amounts of gray-brown streaking on the head and neck. Iceland gulls dabble and dive in the water or pick food from the ground and can be seen scavenging at refuse piles. The winter nonbreeding adult is illustrated.

Glaucous Gull, *Larus hyperboreus*
Family Laridae (Gulls, Terns)
Size: 27"
Season: Winter
Habitat: Open ocean, coastal areas

After breeding in the Arctic, glaucous gulls are winter visitors to New England. They are large, stocky, heavy-set gulls with heavy but straight bills that lack a pronounced angle on the lower mandible. It takes four years to achieve adult plumage, but at all stages it is quite pale, has pinkish legs, and lacks dark patches on the primaries. Breeding adults are very pale gray above and have yellow eyes and a yellow bill with a red spot. Winter adults show faint smudging about the head and neck, are white overall with variable amounts of brown streaking, and have a pale-pinkish, black-tipped bill. The juvenile (top) and winter adult (bottom) are illustrated.

Great Black-backed Gull,
Larus marinus
Family Laridae (Gulls, Terns)
Size: 29"
Season: Year-round
Habitat: Coastal beaches, rocky shores, estuaries

The great black-backed gull is the largest gull worldwide, with an accompanying large head and bill. The plumage is white with a dark, slate-gray back and wings marked with white-edged tertials and secondaries and tips of the outer primaries. The bill is yellow with a red spot on the lower mandible, and the legs are pink. The winter adult has minimal gray streaking on the top part of the head, and juveniles show extensive mottling and spotting on the back and breast. They feed and scavenge on almost anything edible, including fish, mammals, birds, eggs, and invertebrates, and will dominate other species in mixed flocks. They will sometimes drop items from the air to crack them open or kill them. The breeding adult is illustrated.

Black-legged Kittiwake,
Rissa tridactyla
Family Laridae (Gulls, Terns)
Size: 17"
Season: Winter
Habitat: Open ocean, rarely at coastal locations

The black-legged kittiwake is a small, mostly ocean-dwelling gull, similar in habits to a fulmar, that breeds in Alaska and northeastern Canada. It has a large head with prominent dark eyes, a thin yellow bill, a slightly notched tail, and short black legs. Breeding adults are white on the head, underparts, and tail. The mantle and upper wings are medium gray, and the wing tips are solid black. Winter plumage is similar, with the addition of a dark patch behind the eye and gray smudging over the nape. Juveniles show a discreet M-shaped black pattern over the upper wings and a black-tipped tail. This bird plunge-dives, picks at the surface, or submerges for fish and invertebrates. Its voice is a sharp *kik* or the sound for which it's named, *kittiwake*. The winter adult is illustrated.

Least Tern, *Sternula antillarum*
Family Laridae (Gulls, Terns)
Size: 9"
Season: Summer
Habitat: Sandy coastal shores

The least tern is the smallest North American tern and the only tern with a yellow bill and legs. It has a black cap and white forehead patch and is pale gray above and white below. The tail is forked, and the bill is tipped with black. Nonbreeding adults have a dark bill and increased white on the front of the cap. In flight the wings are relatively narrow and there is a black bar on the outer primaries. Least terns often hover over the water before plunge-diving to catch small fish. They also pick worms and insects from the ground. This sensitive bird was once threatened by development of its coastal, sandy breeding grounds. The breeding adult is illustrated.

Caspian Tern, *Sterna caspia*
Family Laridae (Gulls, Terns)
Size: 21"
Season: Summer; spring and fall migrant
Habitat: Coastal areas, river basins

The Caspian tern is a very large, thick-necked tern, the size of a big gull. It has a pointed, rich-red bill that is dark at the tip and a black cap on its head. The upperparts are very pale gray, the underparts are white, and the primary feathers are pale gray above and tipped with dark on the underside. The legs are short and black. Nonbreeding adults have pale streaks through the cap. In flight the Caspian tern uses ponderous, shallow wing beats and is less agile than smaller terns. It flies above the water surface searching for prey, plunging headfirst to snatch small fish, and may rob food from other birds. Its voice is a harsh *craw!* The breeding adult is illustrated.

Roseate Tern, *Sterna dougallii*
Family Laridae (Gulls, Terns)
Size: 12.5"
Season: Summer
Habitat: Sandy or rocky offshore islands, barrier beaches, open ocean

The roseate tern is a medium-size, very pale tern with short, red legs, a rounded crown, a long, forked tail, and a thin bill. The body is white below and pale gray on the back and upperwings, with darker-gray outer primaries, and a crisp, black cap. Breeding adults have a subtle, rosy wash to the breast, giving this bird its name. Winter adults have a white forehead but retain a streaky cap behind the eyes and have darker legs. The bill is solid black most of the year, but the basal half becomes reddish orange in midsummer. Roseate terns feed primarily on small fish, which they catch by plunge-diving from a great height or by snatching them on the water's surface. They voice a two-part, raspy *che-WIT* or a single *keer* call. The nonbreeding adult (top) and breeding adult (bottom) are illustrated.

Common Tern, *Sterna hirundo*
Family Laridae (Gulls, Terns)
Size: 12"
Season: Spring–fall
Habitat: Sandy coastal areas, offshore
islands, inland freshwater wetlands

The common tern is indeed common and widespread across North America, breeding on the North Atlantic coast and wintering in South America. The body shape is similar to the other medium-size terns such as roseate, Arctic, and Forster's, with short, red legs, a streamlined body, and a thin, pointed, red bill. The tail on the common tern is long and deeply forked but does not extend beyond the wingtips on the perched bird. Plumage is white below with a gray wash on the breast and belly, light gray above and on the upperwings, with a neat, black cap atop the head. In flight there is a noticeable dark edge to the primaries. Winter birds (rarely seen in New England) have black bills and legs, a white forehead, and a dark bar on the leading edge of the inner wing. It is sometimes called the "sea swallow" for its graceful flight. The adult is illustrated.

GULLS, TERNS

Arctic Tern, *Sterna paradisaea*
Family Laridae (Gulls, Terns)
Size: 12"
Season: Spring–fall
Habitat: Shorelines, beaches; open
ocean in migration

The Arctic tern is well known for its lengthy migration; it travels up to 25,000 miles round trip from its breeding grounds in the Arctic to its winter habitat in the Antarctic seas. It is a small, short-necked, pale tern with very short legs, a long, forked tail, and a small, pointed bill. Its breeding plumage is light gray overall with a white tail, underwing, and face. There is a solid black cap on the head, and the bill and legs are red. The nonbreeding adult has black legs and bill and a white forehead. In flight note the uniformly pale wings with a thin black trailing edge to the primaries, and thin black outer edges to the tail. The breeding adult is illustrated.

Forster's Tern, *Sterna forsteri*
Family Laridae (Gulls, Terns)
Size: 14"
Season: Spring–fall
Habitat: Coastal areas, lakes, marshes

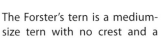

The Forster's tern is a medium-size tern with no crest and a relatively long, pointed orange bill with a black tip. Breeding plumage is very pale gray above and white below, with a forked white tail and very light primaries. The head has a black cap, and the short legs are red. Nonbreeding adults have darker primaries, a black ear patch in place of the cap, and an all-black bill. Forster's terns display swallow-like flight, with narrow pointed wings, and they plunge-dive for fish. They voice short, harsh, one-syllable calls. The nonbreeding adult (top) and breeding adult (bottom) are illustrated.

Black Tern, *Chlidonias niger*
Family Laridae (Gulls, Terns)
Size: 9.5"
Season: Summer resident, migrant in spring and fall
Habitat: Wet meadows, marshes, fields

The black tern is a small, dark tern with a very short, notched tail, and a small, thin, black bill. The breeding adult is dark gray above and black below, with white undertail coverts and vent. The head is all black, and there is a hint of red at the base of the mouth. The tern's nonbreeding plumage is lighter gray above and all white below, with a white head except for black around the eye and at the rear of the crown. Black terns fly low over the water, or circle and hover, dropping down to capture insects, fish, and invertebrates. They do not plunge-dive like other terns. The breeding adult is illustrated.

Black Skimmer, *Rynchops niger*
Family Laridae (Gulls, Terns)
Size: 18"
Season: Summer
Habitat: Coastal bays, estuaries, or inland freshwater rivers and lakes

The black skimmer has a most unique bill, in that the lower mandible is substantially longer than the upper. The red bill is also thick at the base and knife-thin toward the end. This aids in the foraging practice of flying just above the water surface, wings held above the body, with the mouth open and the lower mandible cutting a furrow through the water. When it encounters something solid, the mouth slams shut and, hopefully, the bird acquires a fish. Plumage is black on the back, wings, and crown and white below. The legs are tiny and red. Nonbreeding adults have a white nape, contiguous with the white of the body. The illustration shows a breeding adult.

Parasitic Jaeger, *Stercorarius parasiticus*
Family Stercorariidae (Jaegers, Skuas)
Size: 19"
Season: Spring and fall migrant
Habitat: Offshore oceanic waters

The parasitic jaeger is so named because of its habit of pursuing and pirating prey from gulls and terns by harassing them until they release their catch. It is an aggressive, agile, acrobatic seabird. The parasitic jaeger may take the form of a dark phase, light phase, or anywhere in between. Light-phase birds are dark above, white on the breast and neck, and have a dark band across the lower neck. They also have a dark-brownish cap and a pale patch at the base of the bill. Dark-phase adults are dark brown overall. In all phases there is a distinct white patch at the base of the primary feathers and protruding, sharply pointed inner tail feathers. Of the jaegers, this is the species most likely to be seen close to the shore. The breeding adult is illustrated.

Dovekie, *Alle alle*
Family Alcidae (Alcids)
Size: 8"
Season: Winter
Habitat: Offshore oceanic waters

Rarely seen from shore, the dovekie is a tiny seabird that inhabits the open North Atlantic and Arctic Oceans when it is not breeding on remote, rocky islands in the Arctic Circle. It is plump and short-bodied with a relatively large head, almost no neck, a short tail, and a blunt, stubby bill. The breeding plumage is white below, cleanly contrasting with the black upperparts, head, breast, and tail. The wings are mostly dark except for a white stripe on the trailing edge of the inner wing and white streaks on the scapulars. Winter adults (most often seen in New England) have a white breast and throat, with white extending behind the eye, forming a dark partial collar on the neck. Dovekies use their compact wings in a flying motion to swim underwater, feeding on small marine invertebrates and plankton. The winter adult is illustrated.

Razorbill, *Alca torda*
Family Alcidae (Alcids)
Size: 17"
Season: Winter
Habitat: Offshore oceanic waters, rocky coastal cliffs

The razorbill is a very distinctive, heavy auk, similar to a murre, that winters offshore in the North Atlantic, coming ashore only to breed. Its body is long with a long tail, narrow wings, a bulky head, and a tall, laterally flattened, blunt-tipped bill bisected by a thin, white stripe. Plumage is white below and on the underwing linings, and black above and on the head, tail, and wings. The secondaries are edged with white, creating a delicate, curved stripe on the wing of the perched bird. Breeding birds have a white line of feathers at the lores and an all-black head, while winter birds lack this line and are white at the throat and rear of the face. Razorbills fly fast and direct and swim deep underwater for small fish and crustaceans. They give a low, croaking call when gathered at their breeding colonies. The breeding adult (bottom) and non-breeding adult (top) are illustrated.

Common Murre, *Uria aalge*
Family Alcidae (Alcids)
Size: 17.5"
Season: Winter
Habitat: Open coastal waters; steep, rocky offshore cliffs

Alcids are the Northern Hemisphere's version of penguins. The common murre is a sleek, thin alcid with a short tail and wings and a sloping forehead leading to a narrow, pointed bill. It is black above and on the head and is white below, with dark webbed feet. In winter plumage the white of the breast extends up to the chin and to the back of the eyes. Common murres dive and swim underwater, propelled by their stiff, short wings, to catch fish and squid. Their voice is a rattling, muffled *murr* sound. They breed in huge crowded colonies on steep, rocky cliffs. The nonbreeding adult (left) and breeding adult (right) are illustrated.

Black Guillemot, *Cepphus grylle*
Family Alcidae (Alcids)
Size: 13"
Season: Year-round
Habitat: Open coastal waters; steep, rocky offshore cliffs

The black guillemot is like an eastern version of the pigeon guillemot of the West Coast. It is compact with a longish neck, rounded head, narrow bill, and red-orange, webbed feet. Breeding plumage is black overall with a conspicuous solid white patch along the upper inner wing. Winter adults are white below, mottled gray and white on the back, and have a white head with variable gray smudging, especially around the eyes and crown. Black guillemots dive for fish and invertebrates in shallower water, propelled by wings and feet. The nonbreeding adult (left) and breeding adult (right) are illustrated.

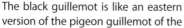

Atlantic Puffin, *Fratercula corniculata*
Family Alcidae (Alcids)
Size: 12.5"
Season: Year-round
Habitat: Offshore islands, open ocean

Also known as the "sea parrot," the Atlantic puffin is a small, compact puffin with short, rounded wings, a short tail, a large head, and a tall, laterally compressed, triangular bill. Its plumage is black above and white below, with a white facial disk, a broad, black collar, and red-orange legs. The bill is blue gray at the base, grooved, and orange on the outer half. In winter the bill is narrower and the face is suffused with sooty gray. Atlantic puffins breed in earthen tunnels on remote islands, where they are quite sociable and docile. They dive underwater from the air or from the surface, and swim to catch small fish (especially sand eels), or crustaceans. When feeding their young, they can carry huge loads of food in there large bills. The adult is illustrated.

Rock Pigeon, *Columba livia*
Family Columbidae (Pigeons, Doves)
Size: 12"
Season: Year-round
Habitat: Urban areas, farmland

Formerly known as the rock dove, the rock pigeon is the common pigeon seen in almost every urban area across the continent. Introduced from Europe, where it inhabits rocky cliffs, rock pigeons have adapted to city life, and domestication has resulted in a wide variety of plumage colors and patterns. The original, wild version is a stocky gray bird with a darker head and neck and green to purple iridescence along the sides of the neck. The eyes are bright red, and the bill has a fleshy white protuberance (cere) on the base of the upper mandible. There are two dark bars across the back when the wing is folded, the rump is white, and the tail has a dark terminal band. Variants range from white to brown to black, with many pattern combinations. The adult is illustrated.

Mourning Dove, *Zenaida macroura*
Family Columbidae (Pigeons, Doves)
Size: 12"
Season: Year-round
Habitat: Open brushy areas, urban areas

The common mourning dove is a sleek, long-tailed dove with a thin neck, a small rounded head, and large black eyes. It is pale gray brown underneath and darker above, with some iridescence to the feathers on the neck. There are clear black spots on the tertials and some coverts, and a dark spot on the upper neck below the eye. The pointed tail is edged with a white band. The mourning dove pecks on the ground for seeds and grains and walks with quick, short steps while bobbing its head. Its flight is strong and direct, and the wings create a whistle as the bird takes off. Its voice is a mournful, owl-like cooing. It is solitary or found in small groups but may form large flocks where food is abundant. The adult is illustrated.

Yellow-billed Cuckoo,
Coccyzus americanus
Family Cuculidae (Cuckoos)
Size: 12"
Season: Summer
Habitat: A variety of woodlands, streamsides, swamps

Like the other cuckoos, the yellow-billed cuckoo is secretive and shy, hiding in vegetation, where it picks insects, caterpillars, and fruit from trees. It is brown above with rufous flight feathers and crisp white below. The bill is yellow with black along the top ridge. The tail is long and gradated with large white spots on the underside. The adult is illustrated.

Black-billed Cuckoo,
Coccyzus erythropthalmus
Family Cuculidae (Cuckoos)
Size: 12"
Season: Summer
Habitat: Woodlands and brushy areas,
often near streams

Usually heard before being seen,
the black-billed cuckoo is a secre-
tive, slow-moving bird. Its body is slim, with a curved, dark-gray
bill and a long, graduated tail with small white tips. The upperparts and wings are brown; underparts are white. The head has
a brown cap that fades to white on the lower face and throat.
Orbital rings are reddish on adults, greenish in juveniles. Black-
billed cuckoos skulk through dense foliage searching for caterpillars, insects, and fruit. Their song is a resonating but monotone
phrase of *coo-coo-coo,* often at night. The adult is illustrated.

Barn Owl, *Tyto alba*
Family Tytonidae (Barn Owls)
Size: 23"
Season: Year-round
Habitat: Barns, farmland, open areas
with mature trees

The barn owl is a large-headed,
pale owl with small dark eyes, a
heart-shaped facial disk, and long,
feathered legs. The wings, back,
tail, and crown are light rusty brown with light-gray smudging
and small white dots. The underside, face, and underwing linings
are white, with spots of rust on the breast. Females are usually
darker than males, with more color and spotting across the breast
and sides. The facial disk is enclosed by a thin line of dark feathers.
Barn owls are nocturnal rodent hunters, and their call is a haunting, raspy *screeee!* The adult male is illustrated.

Eastern Screech-Owl,
Megascops asio
Family Strigidae (Typical Owls)
Size: 8.5"
Season: Year-round
Habitat: Wooded areas or parks, places where cavity-bearing trees exist

The eastern screech-owl is a small, big-headed, eared owl with a short tail and bright-yellow eyes. The highly camouflaged plumage ranges from reddish to brown to gray, depending on the region, but the red form is most common in the East. It is darker above and streaked and barred below. The ear tufts may be drawn back to give a rounded-head appearance, and the bill is grayish green tipped with white. White spots on the margins of the coverts and scapulars create two white bars on the folded wing. It is a nocturnal bird, hunting during the night for small mammals, insects, or fish. Its voice is a descending whistling call or a rapid staccato of one pitch. The red morph adult is illustrated.

Short-eared Owl, *Asio flammeus*
Family Strigidae (Typical Owls)
Size: 15"
Season: Year-round
Habitat: Open country, marshes

Worldwide in distribution, the short-eared owl is a medium-size, large-headed owl with long wings and short, inconspicuous ear tufts. Plumage is mottled brown across the back and wings and is whitish (in males) or buff (in females) underneath with brown streaking down the breast. The facial disk is well formed, with bright-yellow eyes surrounded by patches of black. When it's in flight, with slow and loping wing beats, note the large, pale patch at the base of the primaries. Short-eared owls are commonly active in twilight hours and fly like harriers, low over fields, in search of small rodents. Its voice is a raspy, barking *chek-chek-chek*. The adult is illustrated.

Long-eared Owl, *Asio otus*
Family Strigidae (Typical Owls)
Size: 15"
Season: Year-round
Habitat: Dense woodlands near clearings or fields

The long-eared owl is a cryptic, nocturnal owl with a slender body, relatively long wings, and conspicuous ear tufts. The plumage is a mottled gray brown above and pale with dark streaking below. The bright-yellow-orange eyes are in the middle of dark, vertical stripes, enclosed in a pale-orange facial disk. They can compress their bodies vertically to appear as part of the tree branches. During the night, using their keen sense of hearing, long-eared owls fly on silent wings to hunt small rodents or birds. Their typical call is a series of low, well-spaced *hoo* notes. The adult is illustrated.

Great Horned Owl, *Bubo virginianus*
Family Strigidae (Typical Owls)
Size: 22"
Season: Year-round
Habitat: Almost any environment, from forests to plains to urban areas

Found throughout North America, the great horned owl is a large, strong owl with an obvious facial disk and sharp, long talons. Plumage is variable: Eastern forms are brown overall with heavy barring, brown face, and white chin patch; western forms are grayer and paler. The prominent ear tufts give the owl its name, and the eyes are large and yellow. The great horned owl has exceptional hearing and sight. It feeds at night, perching on branches or posts and then swooping down on silent wings to catch birds, snakes, or mammals up to the size of a cat. The voice is a low *hoo-hoo-hoo*. The adult is illustrated.

Barred Owl, *Strix varia*
Family Strigidae (Typical Owls)
Size: 21"
Season: Year-round
Habitat: Wooded swamps,
upland forests

The barred owl is a large, compact owl with a short tail and wings, rounded head, and big, dark eyes. It lacks the ear tufts seen on the great horned owl and has comparatively small talons. Plumage is gray brown overall with dark barring on the neck and breast, turning to streaking on the belly and flanks. It swoops from its perch to catch small rodents, frogs, or snakes. Its voice, often heard during the day, is a hooting *who-cooks-for-you* or a kind of bark. Its nests are made in tree cavities vacated by other species. The adult is illustrated.

Snowy Owl, *Bubo scandiacus*
Family Strigidae (Typical Owls)
Size: 23"
Season: Winter
Habitat: Open grasslands

The snowy owl is a large owl of the North with a smooth, domed head, feathered feet, and golden-yellow eyes. The plumage of the male is nearly pure white overall, only lightly spotted with black on the back and crown, and barred on the breast with gray. Females and juveniles have more-extensive dark markings but always show a white face. Snowy owls are most active at twilight, swooping down to snatch small mammals or birds, favoring lemmings, especially on their breeding grounds. The adult male is illustrated.

Northern Saw-whet Owl,
Aegolius acadicus
Family Strigidae (Typical Owls)
Size: 8"
Season: Year-round
Habitat: Coniferous or mixed woodlands

The northern saw-whet owl is a very small, compact owl with a big head, large yellow-orange eyes, and a very short tail. Adults are brown above, with spotting along the scapulars and wing coverts. Underparts are white, with thick brown streaking across the breast and sides. The facial disk lacks an obvious dark border, and the bill is black. Juveniles are blackish brown above and plain rufous below, with a distinct white patch on the forehead. Saw-whet owls stay hidden in trees by day and forage during the night for small rodents. The voice is a repeating series of short, high *hoo* notes. The adult is illustrated.

Northern Hawk Owl, *Surnia ulula*
Family Strigidae (Typical Owls)
Size: 16"
Season: Winter
Habitat: Open woodlands and forest edges

The northern hawk owl is a fierce-looking owl of the northern forests with relatively pointed wings and a distinctive, long, pointed tail. Adults are dark brown above with white spotting on the back and wings, and white below, with extensive, thin, brown barring. The facial disk is whitish and bordered on the sides with dark brown. The eyes and bill are yellow. Northern hawk owls are primarily active during the day, feeding on small mammals and birds. The adult is illustrated.

Boreal Owl, *Aegolius funereus*
Family Strigidae (Typical Owls)
Size: 10"
Season: Winter
Habitat: Mixed forests

The boreal owl is a small owl of northern latitudes with a relatively large, flattish head and small, yellow eyes. The white facial disk is framed by black, and the forehead is black with extensive white dotting. The body is brownish with white spotting above and white streaked with brown below. Active at dusk or night, the boreal owl attacks small mammals or insects by flying down from a perch, and voices a series of low-pitched, staccato toots, sometimes of extended duration. Its small size, nocturnal nature, and preference for wooded areas often make this owl difficult to spot. The adult is illustrated.

Common Nighthawk,
Chordeiles minor
Family Caprimulgidae (Nightjars, Nighthawks)
Size: 9"
Season: Summer
Habitat: Variety of habitats including forests, marshes, plains, urban areas

The common nighthawk is primarily nocturnal but may often be seen flying during the day and evening hours, catching insects on the wing with bounding flight. It is cryptically mottled gray, brown, and black, with strong barring on an otherwise pale underside. In the male a white breast band is evident. The tail is long and slightly notched, and the wings are long and pointed, extending past the tail in the perched bird. In flight there is a distinct white patch on both sides of the wings. During the day it is usually seen roosting on posts or branches with its eyes closed. Its voice is a short, nasal, buzzing sound. The adult male is illustrated.

Chuck-will's-widow,

Caprimulgus carolinensis
Family Caprimulgidae (Nightjars, Nighthawks)
Size: 12"
Season: Summer
Habitat: Woodland areas with clearings

Chuck-will's-widow is a highly camouflaged, fairly large nightjar with a fat head, big, dark eyes, and a tiny bill. The body is thick and broad around the midsection, giving a hunched appearance. It is overall rusty or brown gray and spotted and streaked with black. There are pale edges to the scapulars and a pale chin stripe above the dark breast. The tail is long and projects beyond the primaries. In flight note the long, pointed wings and white on the outer tail feathers in the male. Chuck-will's-widow is nocturnal, feeding at night by springing from its perch or the ground for flying insects. During the day it roosts on the ground or in trees with its eyes closed. Its voice is somewhat like its name, *chuck-wil-wi-dow*. The adult is illustrated.

Whip-poor-will,

Caprimulgus vociferus
Family Caprimulgidae (Nightjars, Nighthawks)
Size: 9.75"
Season: Summer
Habitat: Open mixed woodlands

The whip-poor-will is a plump, compact nightjar that roosts during the day and catches flying insects by night. It has large black eyes and a short but wide bill. The plumage is highly cryptic; mottled gray, brown, and black overall with a light-gray patch across the shoulder and a whitish band on the breast. Most easily noticed in flight, males have distinctive white corners on the otherwise dark tail; females have smaller, buff corners. Its voice, as its common name suggests, is a repeating *whip-poor-will,* rising in pitch toward the end. The adult male is illustrated.

Chimney Swift, *Chaetura pelagica*
Family Apodidae (Swifts)
Size: 5"
Season: Summer
Habitat: Variety of habitats including woods, scrub, swamps, urban areas

The gregarious chimney swift is unrelated to the swallows but similar in shape. The body is like a fat torpedo with a very short tail and long, pointed, bowed wings that bend close to the body. It is dark brown overall and slightly paler underneath and at the chin. Constantly on the wing, it catches insects in flight with quick wing beats and fast glides. It never perches but roosts at night on vertical cliffs, trees, or in chimneys. Its voice is a quick chattering uttered in flight. The adult is illustrated.

Ruby-throated Hummingbird, *Archilochus colubris*
Family Trochilidae (Hummingbirds)
Size: 3.5"
Season: Summer
Habitat: Areas with flowering plants, gardens, urban feeders

The ruby-throated hummingbird is a small, delicate bird able to hover on wings that beat at a blinding speed. The long, needle-like bill is used to probe deep into flowers so the bird can lap up the nectar. Its feet are tiny and its body is white below and green above. Males have a dark-green crown and iridescent red throat, or gorget. Females lack the colored gorget and have a light-green crown and white-tipped tail feathers. Their behavior is typical of hummingbirds, hovering and buzzing from flower to flower, emitting chits and squeaks. Most of these birds migrate across the Gulf of Mexico to South America in the winter. The adult male (bottom) and an adult female (top) are illustrated.

Calliope Hummingbird,
Stellula calliope
Family Trochilidae (Hummingbirds)
Size: 3.25"
Season: Summer
Habitat: Brushy fields, feeders

The smallest breeding bird in North America, and an uncommon visitor to New England, the calliope hummingbird is a tiny, short-tailed, and short-billed hummingbird with wings that extend beyond the tail when perched. The adult male is iridescent green above, on the head, and along the sides, while below it is white with an iridescent-red, streaked gorget (sometimes held stiffly away from the body). Females are green above, buff below, with sparse, dark streaking on the throat. Although a tiny bird, the calliope hummingbird makes an arduous migration to wintering grounds in Mexico each year. It feeds on flower nectar or feeders from a hover, or hunts small insects in midair. Its voice is a quick, high-pitched *zip* and buzzy chattering. The female (top) and male (bottom) are illustrated.

Belted Kingfisher,
Megaceryle alcyon
Family Alcedinidae (Kingfishers)
Size: 13"
Season: Year-round
Habitat: Creeks, lakes, sheltered coastline

The widespread but solitary belted kingfisher is a stocky, large-headed bird with a powerful long bill and shaggy crest. It is a grayish blue green above and white below, with a thick blue band across the breast and white dotting on the back. White spots are at the lores. The female has an extra rufous breast band and is rufous along the flanks. Belted kingfishers feed by springing from a perch along the water's edge or by hovering above the water and then plunging headfirst to snatch fish, frogs, or tadpoles. Its flight is uneven, and its voice is a raspy, rattling sound. The adult female is illustrated.

Red-headed Woodpecker,

Melanerpes erythrocephalus
Family Picidae (Woodpeckers)
Size: 9"
Season: Summer
Habitat: Woodlands, areas with standing dead trees, suburbs

The red-headed woodpecker has a striking bright-red head and a powerful, tapered bill. It is black above with a large patch of white across the lower back and secondaries and white below. The juvenile has a pale-brown head and incomplete white back patch. In all woodpeckers the tail is very stiff with sharp tips to aid in support while clinging to a tree trunk. To feed, it pecks at bark for insects but may also fly out to snatch its prey in midair. Nuts will also be taken and stored in tree cavities for winter. This species has been losing nesting cavities since the introduction of the European starling. The adult is illustrated.

Red-bellied Woodpecker,

Melanerpes carolinus
Family Picidae (Woodpeckers)
Size: 9"
Season: Year-round
Habitat: Woodlands, wooded swamps, parks, urban areas

The red-bellied woodpecker is a fairly common, large-billed woodpecker with extensively barred back and wings. The underparts are pale buff with a barely discernable hint of rose on the belly that gives the bird its name. The crown and nape are reddish orange. Females lack the red crown, and juveniles have an entirely gray head. Like all woodpeckers, the red-bellied woodpecker has two toes pointing forward and two toes pointing back to allow a secure grip on tree trunks as it pecks away bark to find insects. It also feeds on nuts and oranges. Its flight is undulating wing beats and glides. The adult is illustrated.

Yellow-bellied Sapsucker, *Sphyrapicus varius*
Family Picidae (Woodpeckers)
Size: 8.5"
Season: Summer
Habitat: Woodlands, swamps, scrub

The sapsuckers are so named for their habit of drilling rows of pits in tree bark, then returning to eat the sap that emerges and the insects that come to investigate. They will also fly-catch and eat berries. The yellow-bellied sapsucker is medium-size with pied black-and-white plumage and barring across the back. The head is boldly patterned black and white with a red crown and red chin (white in females). The belly is unbarred and pale yellow, while the surrounding flanks are white with black barring. In flight there is a distinct white patch on the upper wing. The adult male is illustrated.

Downy Woodpecker,
Picoides pubescens
Family Picidae (Woodpeckers)
Size: 6.5"
Season: Year-round
Habitat: Woodlands, parks in urban areas, streamsides

The downy woodpecker is a tiny woodpecker with a small bill and a relatively large head. It is white underneath with no barring, has black wings barred with white, and has a patch of white on the back. The head is boldly patterned black and white, and the male sports a red nape patch. The base of the bill joins the head with fluffy nasal tufts. Juveniles may show some red on the forehead and crown. Downy woodpeckers forage for berries and insects in the bark and among the smaller twigs of trees. The very similar hairy woodpecker is larger, with a longer bill and more aggressive foraging behavior, sticking to larger branches and not clinging to twigs. The adult male is illustrated.

Hairy Woodpecker, *Picoides villosus*

Family Picidae (Woodpeckers)
Size: 9"
Season: Year-round
Habitat: Mixed woodlands, streamsides near large trees

The hairy woodpecker is very similar in plumage to the downy woodpecker but is larger and has a heavier bill. Also, it pecks for insects in tree bark or on larger branches and will not feed from smaller twigs, as does the downy. It is mostly black above with a white patch on the back and outer tail feathers and some white spotting on the wings. The underside is white with no barring. The head is patterned black and white, and there are small nasal tufts. Males show a red patch on the back of the crown. The voice includes a high-pitched, squeaky *chip-chip,* as well as loud drumming. The adult female is illustrated.

American Three-toed Woodpecker, *Picoides dorsalis*

Family Picidae (Woodpeckers)
Size: 8.75"
Season: Year-round
Habitat: Coniferous forests of higher elevations, especially areas with dead trees

The American three-toed woodpecker is a medium-size, stocky, shy woodpecker with only three toes on each foot. Adults are black above and on the head, with variable amounts of white barring on the back and flight feathers. Underparts are white with gray barring, and the outer tail feathers are white. The head has white stripes behind the eye and above the malar area. Males show a yellow patch on the crown (as do juveniles) and have larger bills than females. Three-toed woodpeckers are mostly quiet but sometimes call out a sharp *jeet!* They feed by picking bark from trees to extract beetles, larvae, and sap. The adult male is illustrated.

Black-backed Woodpecker, *Picoides arcticus*
Family Picidae (Woodpeckers)
Size: 9"
Season: Year-round
Habitat: Coniferous forests, recently burned areas

The black-backed woodpecker is closely related to the American three-toed woodpecker, which has a similar range and also shares the trait of having only three toes on each foot (two pointing forward and one pointing back). The body is stout with a large head and a long, deep-based bill. The upperparts are glossy black and unmarked except for some white bars on the primaries, and white outer tail feathers on an otherwise black tail. The underparts are white with dark-gray barring on the sides, and the throat and lower face are white, split by a dark malar stripe. The upper head is solid black on females, while males and juveniles have a bright-yellow crown patch. They use their strong bills to peck away tree bark to find insect larvae, especially that of beetles, commonly from trees affected by fire. The voice includes a quick *chik* call, various jumbled notes, and drumming. The adult male is illustrated.

Northern Flicker, *Colaptes auratus*
Family Picidae (Woodpeckers)
Size: 12.5"
Season: Summer
Habitat: Variety of habitats including suburbs and parks

The common northern flicker is a large, long-tailed wood-pecker often seen foraging on the ground for ants and other small insects. It is barred brown and black across the back and is buff with black spotting below. The head is brown with a gray nape and crown, and the upper breast carries a prominent half-circle of black. The male has a black patch at the malar region. Flight is undulating and shows an orange wing lining and white rump. This flicker voices a loud, sharp *keee* and will sometimes drum its bill repeatedly at objects, like a jackhammer. The northern flicker is sometimes referred to as the red-shafted flicker. The male is illustrated.

Pileated Woodpecker, *Dryocopus pileatus*
Family Picidae (Woodpeckers)
Size: 16.5"
Season: Year-round
Habitat: Old-growth forests, urban areas with large trees

The pileated woodpecker is North America's largest woodpecker, except for the huge, probably extinct ivory-billed woodpecker. It is powerful, long-necked, and crested. The body is all black, though the primaries have a white base, which is mostly covered in the folded wing. The head is boldly patterned black and white and has a bright-red crest that is limited on the female. The male has a red malar patch, while the female's is black. In flight the contrasting white wing lining can be seen. To forage, pileated woodpeckers chip away chunks of bark to uncover ants and beetles but will feed on berries during the winter months. Their voice is a high-pitched, uneven, resounding *wok-wok-wok*. The adult male is illustrated.

PASSERINES

Olive-sided Flycatcher,

Contopus cooperi
Family Tyrannidae (Tyrant Flycatchers)
Size: 7.5"
Season: Summer
Habitat: Open coniferous woodlands

The olive-sided flycatcher is a stocky flycatcher with a relatively large head, thick neck, and short, slightly notched tail. It is dark olive gray above, on the head, and on the sides, while a white strip runs down the middle of the belly and up to the chin, forming a sort of "vest" shape. The sides of the rump are white, but this is usually concealed in the perched bird. The bill is stout, thick at the base, and pointed. Olive-sided flycatchers perch on high, bare treetop branches and "fly-catch" for insects, grabbing their prey while on the wing. Their voice is a high-pitched *whip-WEE-weer,* sometimes dubbed "quick three beers." The adult is illustrated.

Eastern Wood-pewee, *Contopus virens*
Family Tyrannidae (Tyrant Flycatchers)
Size: 6.25"
Season: Summer
Habitat: Woodland edges, canyons, creek sides

The eastern wood-pewee is a large-headed, thick-necked flycatcher with drab plumage overall. It is brownish gray or olive gray, with pale whitish or dusky underparts and gray sides that meet at the breast. A very slight eye ring surrounds the dark eye, and the bill is thin, pointed, and has a pale lower mandible. There are thin wing bars along the coverts and edges of the tertials. It is nearly identical to the western wood-pewee, but the ranges do not normally overlap. Eastern wood-pewees fly-catch for insects, starting from a high perch and then returning to the same spot. Its voice is composed of shrill, high-pitched *pee-wee* notes. The adult is illustrated.

Yellow-bellied Flycatcher,
Empidonax flaviventris
Family Tyrannidae (Tyrant Flycatchers)
Size: 5.5"
Season: Summer
Habitat: Coniferous forests, bogs

The yellow-bellied flycatcher is a small member of the empid group of flycatchers, with a plump body, a relatively short tail, a broad head, rounded crown, and a short bill. The upperparts are olive to greenish gray with blackish wings that have distinct white wing bars and edges to the tertials and secondaries. The belly and throat are pale to bright yellow (sometimes becoming quite faded), separated by a darker-olive breast. The bill is dark on the upper mandible and pale yellow on the lower mandible, and the eyes are surrounded by a bold, white eye ring. Yellow-bellied flycatchers are secretive in nature, tending to stay in the leafy understory, picking for insects on the ground or catching them in midair. Their voice is a sharp, high *che-wit,* or a softer, rising *pa-wee.* The adult is illustrated.

Acadian Flycatcher, *Empidonax virescens*
Family Tyrannidae (Tyrant Flycatchers)
Size: 6"
Season: Summer
Habitat: Wooded riparian areas

The Acadian flycatcher is a member of the sometimes-confusing *Empidonax* group that breeds throughout the eastern United States. It has a relatively long, robust bill, long wings, a thin eye ring, and often the hind crown shows a slight peak. Its color is olive green above and whitish below with variable amounts of pale-yellow wash on the lower belly and a faint greenish breast band. The wings are dark with pale wing bars and edges to the tertials. Both sexes and juveniles are similar. Acadian flycatchers fly-catch for insects within the tree canopy, and may also eat berries. The song is a high-pitched, sharp *peet-see,* rising on the second syllable. The adult is illustrated.

Least Flycatcher, *Empidonax minimus*
Family Tyrannidae (Tyrant Flycatchers)
Size: 5.25"
Season: Summer
Habitat: Deciduous woodland edges, rural areas, orchards

The least flycatcher is the smallest member of the empid group of flycatchers and one of the most common across the United States. It is similar in shape to the yellow-bellied flycatcher, with a compact body, large head, short tail, mostly rounded crown, short wings, and a short bill. The color, however, is quite drab, being gray to olive gray above and whitish on the throat and underparts (often with a gray wash to the breast and a very pale-yellow wash on the belly). The wings are blackish, with distinct white bars and edges to the tertials and secondaries. The bill is two-toned, black on the upper mandible and yellowish on the lower, and the eye has a complete white eye ring. The sexes are similar, and juveniles show brownish wing bars. They fly from a low perch to snatch insects in midair or off leaves and branches. The voice is similar to the yellow-bellied, with its most common call a sharp, short *cha-wit,* but slightly higher in pitch. The adult is illustrated.

Willow Flycatcher,
Empidonax traillii
Family Tyrannidae (Tyrant Flycatchers)
Size: 5.75"
Season: Summer
Habitat: Moist, brushy areas with willows and foothill fields

The willow flycatcher is similar to many flycatchers in the genus *Empidonax*. It has a crown that peaks at the rear of the head and a fairly thick bill. Its plumage is a greenish brown gray above with pale, dusky underparts and a whitish chin and throat. A thin white eye ring circles the eye, the lores are light, and the lower mandible is pale orange. Distinct wing bars are visible on the folded wing. Willow flycatchers catch insects while in flight, starting from a perch and then returning to the same spot. Their voice is a high, nasal *fitz-bee* call. The adult is illustrated.

Eastern Phoebe, *Sayornis phoebe*
Family Tyrannidae (Tyrant Flycatchers)
Size: 7"
Season: Summer
Habitat: Brushy streamsides

The eastern phoebe is a compact, large-headed flycatcher with a thin, pointed bill and a long tail that it habitually pumps up and down. The plumage is grayish across the back, wings, tail, and head, with darker areas on the face and crown. The underparts are white, sometimes washed with pale yellow on the belly, with a bit of gray extending onto the sides of the breast. The wing bars are quite dull, and there is no distinct eye ring. Sexes are similar, and juveniles show more yellow on the underparts. Eastern phoebes fly-catch for insects from branch tips or fence wires, and sing a song that sounds somewhat like its name, *fee-bee,* or a series of chattering *sit* notes. The adult is illustrated.

Great Crested Flycatcher,

Myiarchus crinitus
Family Tyrannidae (Tyrant Flycatchers)
Size: 8.5"
Season: Summer
Habitat: Open woodlands and scrub, urban areas

The great crested flycatcher is a large flycatcher with a proportionately large head and full crest. The upperparts and head are olive brown, and the throat and breast are gray with a bright-yellow belly. The primaries and tail show rufous color, while the margins to the tertials and coverts are white. Both sexes and the juvenile are similar in plumage. In flight note the yellow wing linings and rufous tail. It feeds by flying from perch to perch, catching insects in flight. It is often seen erecting its crown feathers and bobbing its head. Its voice is a high-pitched, whistling *wheeeeerup!* The adult is illustrated.

Eastern Kingbird,

Tyrannus tyrannus
Family Tyrannidae (Tyrant Flycatchers)
Size: 8.5"
Season: Summer
Habitat: Open woodlands, agricultural and rural areas

The eastern kingbird is a slender, medium-size flycatcher. Its upperparts are bluish black, and its underparts are white with a pale-gray breast. The dark head cap contrasts with the white lower half of the face. The tail is black with a white terminal band. It flies with shallow wing beats on wings that are mostly dark and pointed. Eastern kingbirds perch on wires, treetops, or posts and take flight to capture insects on the wing. The voice is a distinctive series of very high-pitched, sputtering, zippy *psit* notes. The adult is illustrated.

Northern Shrike,
Lanius excubitor
Family Laniidae (Shrikes)
Size: 10"
Season: Winter
Habitat: Dry open country

The northern shrike is raptor-like
in its feeding habits. It swoops down from a perch on a branch, wire, or post and captures large insects, small mammals, or birds, impaling them on thorny barbs before tearing them apart to feed. It has a compact, large head and a medium-length, thick, moderately hooked bill. The upperparts are light gray with a white rump, and the underparts are pale and finely barred. The wings are black, with white patches at the base of the primaries and upper coverts. The tail is black and edged with white. There is a black mask on the head extending from the base of the bill to the ear area, but this does not extend above the eye. It flies with quick wing beats and swooping glides. The adult is illustrated.

White-eyed Vireo, *Vireo griseus*
Family Vireonidae (Vireos)
Size: 5"
Season: Summer
Habitat: Dense woodlands, thickets, shrubs

The white-eyed vireo is a small, chunky vireo with a relatively large head and short bill. It is grayish olive green above and pale gray below, tinged with yellow on the flanks and undertail coverts. The head is grayish with conspicuous yellow "spectacles," or combined lores and eye-ring area. The large eye is white. On the wings are two white wing bars. The juvenile bird has a darker eye than that of the adult. This bird gleans insects, spiders, and berries from the dense vegetation. The adult is illustrated.

Yellow-throated Vireo,
Vireo flavifrons
Family Vireonidae (Vireos)
Size: 5.5"
Season: Summer
Habitat: High canopy in mature, moist, mixed woodlands

The yellow-throated vireo is a compact vireo with a short tail. It has olive and gray upperparts with a bright-yellow chin and breast fading to a white belly and undertail region. Yellow "spectacles" encompass the dark eyes. There are two distinct white wing bars on the wing coverts. It gleans insects and berries from leaves high in the canopy. The adult is illustrated.

Blue-headed Vireo,
Vireo solitarius
Family Vireonidae (Vireos)
Size: 5.5"
Season: Summer
Habitat: Woodland, urban areas with trees

The blue-headed vireo was once grouped with the Plumbeous and Cassin's vireos as one species, the solitary vireo. It is olive gray above and white below, tinged with yellow on the sides and flanks. The head is blue gray with white "spectacles" and a white chin. There are two white or pale-yellow wing bars on the wing coverts. It gleans insects and berries in the upper tree canopies. Its voice consists of short, high-pitched phrases. The adult is illustrated.

Red-eyed Vireo,
Vireo olivaceus
Family Vireonidae (Vireos)
Size: 6"
Season: Summer
Habitat: Areas of dense vegetation, mature deciduous forests

The red-eyed vireo is a sluggish, slow-moving bird that haunts the upper tree canopy picking out insects and berries. Its head appears rather flat, and its tail is short. It is light olive green above and white below, with a yellow wash across the breast, flanks, and undertail coverts. It has a dark eye line, white eyebrow, and a grayish crown. The eyes are red, and the bill is fairly large with a hooked tip. The voice is a repetitive, incessant song in single phrases. The adult is illustrated.

Warbling Vireo, *Vireo gilvus*
Family Vireonidae (Vireos)
Size: 5.5"
Season: Summer
Habitat: Moist deciduous woodlands, parks

The warbling vireo is a plain, light-colored, stocky vireo with a fairly short, hooked bill. The upperparts are pale brownish or greenish gray with no distinct wing bars, and the underside is whitish or washed with pale yellow brown. The dark eyes contrast with the light superciliary stripes and lores. The underside of the wing is two-toned with light linings and darker flight feathers. Warbling vireos forage in trees for insects and berries and sing a high-pitched, warbling song. The adult is illustrated.

Philadelphia Vireo,
Vireo philadelphicus
Family Vireonidae (Vireos)
Size: 6"
Season: Summer
Habitat: Deciduous woodlands, especially with second-growth trees such as alder

The Philadelphia vireo is a small, stocky vireo, similar in structure to a chubby warbling vireo (which shares its range), with a short tail, short bill, and a rounded crown, not unlike the shape of a large warbler. The color is drab, olive-gray above and on the wings, with no evident wing bars, lemon yellow below and on the throat, and often whitish on the belly. The white central face region is bisected by a gray-brown eye stripe and topped with a relatively dark crown. The sexes are similar. They hunt primarily insects by snatching them in midair or from leaves and branches; they will also occasionally eat small fruits. The voice is a musical, high-pitched series of three to four syllables with a moderate pause in between. The adult is illustrated.

Gray Jay, *Perisoreus canadensis*
Family Corvidae (Jays, Crows)
Size: 11.5"
Season: Year-round
Habitat: Coniferous forests, mountainous areas

Bold and inquisitive, the gray jay (also known as the Canada jay or camp robber) is a fluffy jay with a long tail and a stubby black bill. The plumage is dark gray above and pale gray to whitish below. The head is white with a variable amount of black on the back of the crown and upper nape. Juveniles are sooty gray overall with a light gray bill and a pale gray malar stripe. Gray jays glean insects, berries, or seeds; raid campsites; and cache food on the bark of trees using their sticky saliva. Their voice is variously sweet or raucous, but they are generally quiet. The adult is illustrated.

Blue Jay, *Cyanocitta cristata*
Family Corvidae (Jays, Crows)
Size: 11"
Season: Year-round
Habitat: Woodlands, rural sites, and urban areas

The solitary blue jay is a sturdy, crested jay. It is bright blue above and white below, with a thick, tapered, black bill. There is a white patch around the eye that extends to the chin, bordered by a thin, black "necklace" extending to the nape. It has a conspicuous white wing bar and dark barring on the wings and tail. In flight the white outer edges of the tail are visible. The jay alternates shallow wing beats with glides. Omnivorous, the blue jay eats just about anything, especially acorns, nuts, fruits, insects, and small vertebrates. It is a raucous and noisy bird and quite bold. Sometimes it mimics the calls of birds of prey. The adult is illustrated.

American Crow,
Corvus brachyrhynchos
Family Corvidae (Jays, Crows)
Size: 17.5"
Season: Year-round
Habitat: Open woodlands, pastures, rural fields, dumps

The American crow is a widespread corvid found across the continent, voicing its familiar, loud, grating *caw-caw*. It is a large, stocky bird with a short, rounded tail, broad wings, and a thick, powerful bill. Plumage is glistening black overall in all stages of development. It will eat almost anything and often forms loose flocks with other crows. The adult is illustrated.

Fish Crow, *Corvus ossifragus*
Family Corvidae (Jays, Crows)
Size: 15"
Season: Year-round
Habitat: Coastal marshes, rivers, agricultural areas

The fish crow is virtually identical to the American crow but is a bit smaller with uniformly glossy plumage and generally stays close to coastal areas. It also has a softer, nasal, *ah-hah* voice and prefers to forage on fish and crustaceans. The adult is illustrated.

Common Raven, *Corvus corax*
Family Corvidae (Jays, Crows)
Size: 24"
Season: Year-round
Habitat: Wide range of habitats including deserts, mountains, canyons, and forests

The common raven is a large, stocky, gruff corvid with a long, massive bill that slopes directly into the forehead. The wings are narrow and long, and the tail is rounded or wedge-shaped. The entire body is glossy black, sometimes bluish, and the neck is laced with pointed, shaggy feathers. Quite omnivorous, it feeds on carrion, refuse, insects, and roadkill. It has a varied voice that includes deep croaking. Ravens may soar and engage in rather acrobatic flight. Crows are similar but are smaller, with proportionately smaller bills. The adult is illustrated.

Horned Lark, *Eremophila alpestris*
Family Alaudidae (Larks)
Size: 7"
Season: Year-round
Habitat: Open and barren country

The horned lark is a slim, elongated, ground-dwelling bird with long wings. The plumage is pale reddish gray above and whitish below, with variable amounts of rusty smudging or streaking on the breast and sides. The head is boldly patterned with a black crown, cheek patch, and breast bar, contrasting with a yellow throat and white face. In females the black markings are much paler. Particularly evident on males are feather tufts, or "horns," on the sides of the crown. The outer tail feathers are black. Horned larks scurry on the ground, foraging for plant matter and insects, and sing with rapid, musical warbles and chips. The adult male is illustrated.

Purple Martin, *Progne subis*
Family Hirundinidae (Swallows)
Size: 8"
Season: Summer
Habitat: Marshes, open water, agricultural areas

The purple martin is the largest North American swallow. It has long, pointed wings, a streamlined body, and a forked tail. The bill is very short and broad at the base. The male is dark overall, with a blackish-blue sheen across the back and head, while the female is paler overall, with sooty, mottled underparts. Purple martins fly with fast wing beats alternating with circular glides. They commonly use man-made nest boxes or tree hollows as nesting sites. The adult male is illustrated.

Tree Swallow, *Tachycineta bicolor*
Family Hirundinidae (Swallows)
Size: 5.75"
Season: Summer
Habitat: Variety of habitats near water and perching sites

The tree swallow has a short, slightly notched tail, broad-based triangular wings, and a thick neck. It has a high-contrast plumage pattern, with upperparts that are dark metallic green blue and crisp-white underparts. When perched, the primaries reach just past the tail tip. Juveniles are gray brown below, with a subtle, darker breast band. Tree swallows take insects on the wing but will also eat berries and fruits. They often form huge lines of individuals perched on wires or branches. Their voice is a high-pitched chirping. The adult is illustrated.

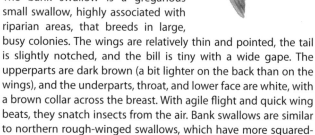

Bank Swallow, *Riparia riparia*
Family Hirundinidae (Swallows)
Size: 5"
Season: Summer
Habitat: Steep, sandy banks along river and pond edges

The bank swallow is a gregarious small swallow, highly associated with riparian areas, that breeds in large, busy colonies. The wings are relatively thin and pointed, the tail is slightly notched, and the bill is tiny with a wide gape. The upperparts are dark brown (a bit lighter on the back than on the wings), and the underparts, throat, and lower face are white, with a brown collar across the breast. With agile flight and quick wing beats, they snatch insects from the air. Bank swallows are similar to northern rough-winged swallows, which have more squared-off tails and only suffuse brown about the breast and lower face. The adult is illustrated.

Northern Rough-winged
Swallow, *Stelgidopteryx serripennis*
Family Hirundinidae (Swallows)
Size: 5.5"
Season: Summer
Habitat: Sandy cliffs, steep streamsides, outcrops, bridges

The northern rough-winged swallow flies in a smooth and even fashion with full wing beats, feeding on insects caught on the wing. It is uniformly brownish above and white below. The breast is lightly streaked with pale brown, and the tail is short and square. Juveniles show light rust-colored wing bars on the upper coverts. These fairly solitary swallows find nesting sites in holes in sandy cliffs. The adult is illustrated.

Cliff Swallow,
Petrochelidon pyrrhonota
Family Hirundinidae (Swallows)
Size: 5.5"
Season: Summer
Habitat: Sandy cliffs, steep streamsides, outcrops, bridges

The cliff swallow is a colonial, active swallow with a short, broad-based bill and a short, squared tail. Adults are dark above and on the wings and tail and have a contrasting buff rump. The underparts are white with dark chestnut across the face and throat, and there is a dark-blue crown fronted by a white forehead. Juveniles are duller and lack the white forehead. Cliff swallows snatch flying insects in midair, flying rapidly with extended glides. They build rounded, vessel-shaped nests made from globs of mud extracted from nearby shores and puddles. The adult is illustrated.

Barn Swallow, *Hirundo rustica*
Family Hirundinidae (Swallows)
Size: 6.5"
Season: Summer
Habitat: Old buildings, caves, open rural areas near bridges

The widespread and common barn swallow has narrow, pointed wings and a long, deeply forked tail. It is pale below and dark blue above with a rusty-orange forehead and throat. The male's underparts are pale orange, while the female's are pale cream. Barn swallows are graceful, fluid fliers, and they often forage in groups to catch insects in flight. They build cup-shaped nests of mud on almost any protected man-made structure. Their voice is a loud, repetitive chirping or clicking. The adult male is illustrated.

Black-capped Chickadee,
Poecile atricapillus
Family Paridae (Chickadees, Titmice)
Size: 5.25"
Season: Year-round
Habitat: Mixed woodlands, rural gardens, feeders

The black-capped chickadee is a small, compact, active bird with short, rounded wings and a tiny black bill. It is gray above and lighter gray or dusky below with a contrasting black cap and throat patch. Its voice sounds like its name—*chick-a-dee, dee, dee*—or is a soft *fee-bay*. It is quite social and feeds on a variety of seeds, berries, and insects found in trees and shrubs. The adult is illustrated.

Boreal Chickadee,
Poecile hudsonicus
Family Paridae (Chickadees, Titmice)
Size: 5.5"
Season: Year-round
Habitat: Coniferous forests

The boreal chickadee is a dark chickadee of northern boreal forests with a plump body, rounded wings, a big head, and a small bill. It is quite similar to the black-capped chickadee, which shares its range, but there are noticeable color differences. The boreal is grayish brown above and on the wings, has a gray nape, and has a rich-brown cap above a white face. The underparts are whitish with cinnamon-brown sides and flanks and a black throat patch. It flits about in dense foliage, often clinging upside down on small branches while feeding on insects, larvae, and seeds. It stashes extra food among bark and needles to eat during lean winter months. Its most common call is a raspy *chick-a-dee* or *chick-a-dee-dee*. The adult is illustrated.

Tufted Titmouse, *Baeolophus bicolor*
Family Paridae (Chickadees, Titmice)
Size: 6.5"
Season: Year-round
Habitat: Woodlands, urban areas

The tame and curious tufted titmouse is a small, chunky bird with short, broad wings and a conspicuous tuft on the crest. It is gray above and pale gray below with a wash of orange along the sides and flanks. It has a small but sturdy black bill, large black eyes, and a black forehead. It often forms foraging groups with other species who flit through the vegetation picking out nuts, seeds, insects, and berries from the bark and twigs. At feeders the tufted titmouse prefers sunflower seeds. Its voice is a repetitive *peeta peeta*. The adult is illustrated.

Brown Creeper, *Certhia americana*
Family Certhiidae (Creepers)
Size: 5.25"
Season: Year-round
Habitat: Mature woodlands

The brown creeper is a small, cryptically colored bird with a long, pointed tail and a long, downcurved bill. It is mottled black, brown, and white above, while below it is a plain white that fades to brownish toward the rear. The face has a pale supercilium and a white chin. The legs are short, with long, grasping toes. Like a woodpecker, it has a stiff tail that aids in propping the bird up. Brown creepers spiral upward on tree trunks, probing for insects in the bark, then fly to the bottom of another tree to repeat the process. Their voice is composed of thin, high-pitched *seet* notes. The adult is illustrated.

White-breasted Nuthatch,
Sitta carolinensis
Family Sittidae (Nuthatches)
Size: 5.75"
Season: Year-round
Habitat: Mixed deciduous and coniferous woodlands

The white-breasted nuthatch has a large head and wide neck, short rounded wings, and a short tail. It is blue gray above and pale gray below, with rusty smudging on the lower flanks and undertail coverts. The breast and face are white, and there is a black crown merging with the mantle. The bill is long, thin, and upturned at the tip. To forage, it creeps headfirst down tree trunks to pick out insects and seeds. It nests in tree cavities high off the ground. Its voice is a nasal, repetitive *auk-auk-auk*. The adult is illustrated.

Red-breasted Nuthatch,

Sitta canadensis
Family Sittidae (Nuthatches)
Size: 4.5"
Season: Year-round
Habitat: Open coniferous and
deciduous forests

The red-breasted nuthatch is
a small, stubby, large-headed,
short-tailed bird with a long, thin, slightly upturned bill. Its plumage is blue gray above and rusty orange or buff (in the female) below. The head is white with a black crown and eye stripe. The legs are short, but the toes are very long to aid in grasping tree bark. Nuthatches creep downward, headfirst, on tree trunks and branches to pick out insects and seeds. Their call is a nasal, repetitive *yonk-yonk-yonk*. The adult is illustrated.

WRENS

Carolina Wren,

Thryothorus ludovicianus
Family Troglodytidae (Wrens)
Size: 5.5"
Season: Year-round
Habitat: Understory of wooded and
brushy areas, swamps

The Carolina wren is a vocal but cryptic bird, usually hidden among dense foliage close to the ground. It lurks in vegetation, picking out insects, seeds, or fruit, emitting a musical song or a harsh, quick call. The body is plump with a short, rounded tail and a thin, slightly downcurved bill. It is dark rusty brown above, buffy below, and has a long, white superciliary stripe extending to the nape. Its wings and tail are thinly barred with black. This bird habitually holds its tail in a cocked-up position. The adult is illustrated.

House Wren, *Troglodytes aedon*
Family Troglodytidae (Wrens)
Size: 4.75"
Season: Summer
Habitat: Shrubby areas, rural gardens

The house wren is a loud, drab wren with short, rounded wings and a thin, pointed, downcurved bill. Plumage is brown and barred above and is pale gray brown below, with barring on the lower belly, undertail coverts, and tail. The head is lighter on the throat, at the lores, and above the eyes. House wrens feed in the brush for insects and sing rapid, melodic, chirping songs, often while cocking their tails downward. The adult is illustrated.

Winter Wren,
Troglodytes hiemalis
Family Troglodytidae (Wrens)
Size: 4"
Season: Year-round
Habitat: Moist woodlands, streams

The winter wren is a tiny, short-tailed, and plump wren that is brown overall with dark mottling and barring. It is a bit paler on the throat and breast and has a distinct pale supercilium. The tail is commonly held cocked up and the bill is held slightly tilted up. It forages through dense vegetation searching for insects. Inquisitive and curious, winter wrens may be lured into view by imitating their high-pitched, buzzy calls. The adult is illustrated.

WRENS

Marsh Wren, *Cistothorus palustris*
Family Troglodytidae (Wrens)
Size: 5"
Season: Summer
Habitat: Marshes, reeds, stream banks

The marsh wren is a small, cryptic, rufous-brown wren with a normally cocked-up tail. The tail and wings are barred with black, and the chin and breast are white. There is a well-defined white superciliary stripe below a uniform brown crown, and the mantle shows distinct black-and-white striping. The bill is long and slightly decurved. Marsh wrens are vocal day and night with quick, repetitive cheeping. They are secretive but inquisitive and glean insects from the marsh vegetation and water surface. The adult is illustrated.

Golden-crowned Kinglet,
Regulus satrapa
Family Regulidae (Kinglets)
Size: 4"
Season: Year-round
Habitat: Mixed woodlands, brushy areas

The golden-crowned kinglet is a tiny, plump songbird with a short tail and a short, pointed bill. It is greenish gray above, with wings patterned in black, white, and green, and is pale gray below. The face has a dark eye stripe and crown, and the center of the crown is golden yellow and sometimes raised. The legs are dark with orange toes. Kinglets are in constant motion, flitting and dangling among branches, sometimes hanging upside down or hovering at the edge of branches to feed. Their voice includes very high-pitched *tzee* notes. The adult is illustrated.

Ruby-crowned Kinglet,
Regulus calendula
Family Regulidae (Kinglets)
Size: 4"
Season: Year-round
Habitat: Mixed woodlands, brushy areas

The ruby-crowned kinglet is a tiny, plump songbird with a short tail and a diminutive, thin bill. It has a habit of nervously twitching its wings as it actively flits through vegetation, gleaning small insects and larvae. It may also hover in search of food. Plumage is pale olive green above and paler below, with patterned wings and pale wing bars on the upper coverts. There are white eye rings or crescents around the eyes. The bright-red crest of the male bird is faintly noticeable unless the crest is raised. Its voice is a very high-pitched, whistling *seeee*. The adult is illustrated.

Blue-gray Gnatcatcher,
Polioptila caerulea
Family Polioptilidae (Gnatcatchers)
Size: 4.5"
Season: Summer
Habitat: Deciduous or pine woodlands and thickets

The blue-gray gnatcatcher is a tiny, energetic, long-tailed bird with a narrow, pointed bill and thin, dark legs. It is blue gray above and pale gray below, with white edges to the tertials that create a light patch on the middle of the folded wing. The tail is rounded and has black inner and white outer feathers. The eye is surrounded by a crisp white eye ring. Males are brighter blue overall and have a darker supraloreal line. To forage, gnatcatchers flit through thickets and catch insects in the air. They will often twitch and fan their tails. Their voice is a high-pitched buzzing or *cheep* sound, sometimes sounding like the calls of other birds. The adult male is illustrated.

Eastern Bluebird, *Sialia sialis*
Family Turdidae (Thrushes)
Size: 7"
Season: Year-round
Habitat: Open woodland, pastures, fields

The eastern bluebird is a member of the thrush family that travels in small groups, feeding on a variety of insects, spiders, and berries, and singing a series of musical *chur-lee* notes. It is a stocky, short-tailed, and short-billed bird that often perches in an upright posture on wires and posts. The male is brilliant blue above and rusty orange below with a white belly and undertail region. The orange extends to the nape, making a subtle collar. The female is paler overall with a white throat and eye ring. Juveniles are brownish-gray with extensive white spotting and barred underparts. Man-made nest boxes have helped this species increase in numbers throughout its range. The adult male (bottom) and female (top) are illustrated.

Veery, *Catharus fuscescens*
Family Turdidae (Thrushes)
Size: 7"
Season: Summer
Habitat: Moist deciduous forests

The veery is a secretive, plain-colored thrush that is more often detected by its voice than its appearance. It is a rich, reddish brown above and whitish below with pale-gray flanks. The breast is washed with light, tawny brown and has pale streaking, while the head is mostly unmarked with a lighter loreal area and slight eye rings. Veeries pick through the undergrowth or on the ground for worms and insects but may also catch flying insects midair. Their song is composed of liquid, descending, fluting notes, and the call sounds similar to its name, *veer-ree*. The adult is illustrated.

Gray-cheeked Thrush,
Catharus minimus
Family Turdidae (Thrushes)
Size: 7.5"
Season: Spring and fall migrant
Habitat: Mixed coniferous and spruce forests, willow thickets

The gray-cheeked thrush has the most northerly range of all thrushes, and was previously considered the same species as the very similar Bicknell's thrush, which also occurs in New England. It is plain gray brown above, has a whitish belly with gray flanks and sides, and the breast is extensively spotted. The cheeks are grayish, and there are indistinct, thin, pale eye rings. This thrush has a particularly long primary extension and pinkish legs. Reclusive in nature, it forages mostly on the ground and undergrowth for berries, insects, and worms. Its song consists of high-pitched, slightly raspy, fluted notes descending at the end. The adult is illustrated.

Hermit Thrush, *Catharus guttatus*
Family Turdidae (Thrushes)
Size: 7"
Season: Summer
Habitat: Woodlands, brushy areas

The hermit thrush is a compact, short-tailed thrush that habitually cocks its tail. It forages on the ground near vegetative cover for insects, worms, and berries, and voices a song of beautiful, flutelike notes. It is reddish to olive brown above with a rufous tail. The underparts are white, with dusky flanks and sides and black spotting on the throat and breast. The dark eyes are encircled by complete white eye rings. In flight the pale wing lining contrasts with the dark flight feathers. The adult is illustrated.

Wood Thrush,
Hylocichla mustelina
Family Turdidae (Thrushes)
Size: 7.75"
Season: Summer
Habitat: Dense, mixed woodlands; suburban areas

The wood thrush is a solitary, fairly plump thrush with a short tail and a relatively large bill. It is rich reddish orange on the head, fading to a duller brown across the back and tail. Below, it is white with extensive dark spotting from the throat down to the flanks. There is a distinct white eye ring and a black-and-white streaked auricular patch. The legs are thin and pale pink. Sexes are similar. Wood thrushes hop through the undergrowth and along the ground for insects, worms, or berries and voice a beautiful, fluting song preceded by short, soft notes. The adult is illustrated.

American Robin, *Turdus migratorius*
Family Turdidae (Thrushes)
Size: 10"
Season: Year-round
Habitat: Widespread in a variety of habitats including woodlands, fields, parks, and lawns

Familiar and friendly, the American robin is a large thrush with a long tail and long legs. It commonly holds its head cocked and keeps its wing tips lowered beneath its tail. It is gray brown above and rufous below, with a darker head and contrasting white eye crescents and loreal patches. The chin is streaked black and white, and the bill is yellow with darker edges. Females are typically paler overall, and juveniles show white spots above and dark spots below. Robins forage on the ground, picking out earthworms and insects or will flit through trees in search of berries. Their song is a series of high musical phrases sounding like *cheery, cheer-u-up, cheerio.* The adult male is illustrated.

Gray Catbird,
Dumetella carolinensis
Family Mimidae (Mockingbirds,
Catbirds, Thrashers)
Size: 8.5"
Season: Summer
Habitat: Understory of woodland
edges, shrubs, rural gardens

The solitary gray catbird is long-necked and sleek with a sturdy, pointed bill. It is uniformly gray except for its rufous undertail coverts, black crown, and black, rounded tail. It is quite secretive and spends most of its time hidden in thickets close to the ground, picking through the substrate for insects, berries, and seeds. Its call includes a nasal, catlike *meew,* from which its name is derived, although it will also mimic the songs of other birds. To escape danger, it will often choose to run away rather than fly. The adult is illustrated.

Northern Mockingbird,
Mimus polyglottos
Family Mimidae (Mockingbirds, Catbirds,
Thrashers)
Size: 10.5"
Season: Year-round
Habitat: Open fields, grassy areas near
vegetative cover, suburbs, parks

The northern mockingbird is constantly vocalizing. Its scientific name, *polyglottos,* means "many voices," alluding to its amazing mimicry of the songs of other birds. Sleek, long-tailed, and long-legged, it shows gray plumage above with darker wings and tail and off-white to brownish gray plumage below. The bird has two white wing bars, short, dark eye stripes, and pale eye rings. In flight it reveals conspicuous white patches on the inner primaries and coverts and white outer tail feathers. Like other mimids, the mockingbird forages on the ground for insects and berries, intermittently flicking its wings. The adult is illustrated.

Brown Thrasher,
Toxostoma rufum
Family Mimidae (Mockingbirds, Catbirds, Thrashers)
Size: 11"
Season: Summer
Habitat: Woodlands, thickets, urban gardens, orchards

The brown thrasher is primarily a ground-dwelling bird that thrashes through leaves and dirt for insects and plant material. It has a long tail and legs with a medium-length, slightly decurved bill. Plumage is rufous brown above, including the tail, and whitish below, heavily streaked with brown or black. There are two prominent, pale wing bars and pale outermost corners to the tail. Its eye is yellow to orange. Its voice is a variety of musical phrases, often sung from a conspicuous perch. The adult is illustrated.

STARLINGS

European Starling, *Sturnus vulgaris*
Family Sturnidae (Starlings)
Size: 8.5"
Season: Year-round
Habitat: Found almost anywhere, particularly in rural fields, gardens, dumps, urban parks

Introduced from Europe, the European starling has successfully infiltrated most habitats in North America and competes with native birds for nest cavities. It is a stocky, sturdy, aggressive bird that is glossy black overall with a sheen of green or purple. The breeding adult has a yellow bill and greater iridescence, while the adult in winter is more flat black, with a black bill and numerous white spots. The tail is short and square. Starlings form very large, compact flocks and fly directly on pointed, triangular wings. Their diet is highly variable and includes insects, grains, and berries. Vocalizations include loud, wheezy whistles and clucks and imitations of other birdsongs. The breeding adult is illustrated.

American Pipit, *Anthus rubescens*
Family Motacillidae (Pipits)
Size: 6.5"
Season: Spring and fall migrant
Habitat: Fields, shorelines

The American pipit is a slim, ground-dwelling, sparrow-size bird with long legs and a thin, pointed bill. It is grayish brown above with pale wing bars; underneath it is buff or whitish with variable amounts of dark streaking down the breast, sides, and flanks. The head is gray brown with a lighter supercilium and malar area. There are white outer tail feathers on an otherwise dark tail. Pipits walk upright in small groups while foraging for insects on the ground and often pump and wag their tails. The American pipit is also known as the water pipit. The adult is illustrated.

Bohemian Waxwing,
Bombycilla garrulus
Family Bombycillidae (Waxwings)
Size: 7"
Season: Winter
Habitat: Woodlands, swamps, urban areas near berry trees

The bohemian waxwing is a compact, crested songbird with pointed wings and a short tail. Plumage is sleek and smooth, brownish gray overall with paler gray underparts and rufous undertail coverts. The head pattern is striking, with a crisp black mask thinly bordered by white. The tail and edges of the primaries are tipped with bright yellow, and the tips of the secondary feathers are coated with a unique, red, waxy substance. Bohemian waxwings will form large flocks and devour berries from a tree, then move on to the next. They may also fly-catch small insects. Their voice is an extremely high-pitched whistling *seee*. The adult is illustrated.

Cedar Waxwing,
Bombycilla cedrorum
Family Bombycillidae (Waxwings)
Size: 7"
Season: Year-round
Habitat: Woodlands, swamps, urban areas near berry trees

Quite similar to the bohemian waxwing, the cedar waxwing is a compact, crested songbird with pointed wings and a short tail. The sleek, smooth plumage is brownish gray overall with paler underparts, a yellowish wash on the belly, and white undertail coverts. The head pattern is striking, with a crisp black mask thinly bordered by white. The tail is tipped with bright yellow, and the tips of the secondary feathers are coated with a unique, red, waxy substance. Cedar waxwings will form large flocks and devour berries from a tree, then move on to the next. They may also catch small insects while in flight. Their voice is an extremely high-pitched, whistling *seee*. The adult is illustrated.

Golden-winged Warbler,
Vermivora chrysoptera
Family Parulidae (Wood-Warblers)
Size: 4.75"
Season: Summer
Habitat: Woodland edges, brushy fields

The golden-winged warbler has a long, thin, sharp bill that it uses to extract and pick insects and larvae. The plumage is gray above and pale gray or whitish below, and there are white outer corners to the tail. Yellow wing coverts create a broad yellow patch on the upper wings. Males have a striking black facial mask and throat with a yellow forecrown. Females are patterned similarly but with a gray mask and throat and a grayer yellow crown. They build a nest in thickets on the ground. The breeding male (bottom) and female (top) are illustrated.

Blue-winged Warbler, *Vermivora pinus*
Family Parulidae (Wood-Warblers)
Size: 4.75"
Season: Summer
Habitat: Open brushy woodlands, woodland edges

The blue-winged warbler is a bright, summer breeder in New England, commonly found in second-growth woodlands, similar in shape and size to the golden-winged warbler, with which it often hybridizes. The body and head are bright yellow with an olive-green nape and back, bluish-gray wings and tail, and white undertail coverts. There are distinct, white wing bars and white patches on the outer tail feathers. The relatively long, pointed bill is black, merging with a crisp, black eye stripe. Females are similar but with a lighter eye stripe and olive green on the crown. They forage in the middle canopy or brush, mainly for insects, sometimes hovering or clinging upside down to small branches. The voice is a drawn-out, harsh, raspy *zeee* followed by a lower rattling note. The adult male is illustrated.

Tennessee Warbler, *Vermivora peregrina*
Family Parulidae (Wood-Warblers)
Size: 4.75"
Season: Summer
Habitat: Mixed woodlands with brushy thickets, bogs

The Tennessee warbler is a somewhat plain-looking warbler that breeds in New England and throughout Canada, with a plump body, short tail, and medium-length, pointed bill. Breeding males are olive green above, grayer on the wings and tail, with unstreaked, white underparts. Pale-green wing bars are present but very subtle. The head and nape are bluish gray with a thin, dark eye line and a white supercilium. Breeding females have a more olive-colored crown and nape and have a yellow wash to the throat and breast. Juveniles and winter adults of both sexes show more yellowish color overall. They often forage high in the canopy, feeding on insects, larvae, or berries, which they glean from foliage, sometimes by hanging upside down on small branches. The voice is a three-part collection of accelerating, high-pitched cheeps. The breeding male (bottom) and female (top) are illustrated.

Orange-crowned Warbler,
Oreothlypis celata
Family Parulidae (Wood-Warblers)
Size: 5"
Season: Spring and fall migrant
Habitat: Mixed woodlands,
brushy thickets

The orange-crowned warbler is rather plain, with a relatively long tail and a thin, pointed bill. It is olive green above and brighter yellow streaked with olive below, and the undertail coverts are solid yellow. It has a short, dark eye line and a thin, pale, broken eye ring. There is much variation in this species, from brighter forms to grayer forms, and the orange crown patch is rarely visible. Orange-crowned warblers forage for insects or berries in the undergrowth and voice a long series of descending staccato *tit* notes. The adult is illustrated.

Nashville Warbler,
Vermivora ruficapilla
Family Parulidae (Wood-Warblers)
Size: 4.5"
Season: Summer
Habitat: Deciduous and mixed
woodlands, brushy areas, riparian
zones, typically in drier areas

The Nashville warbler is a stocky, big-headed, bright warbler with a relatively short, rounded tail. Sexes are similar, with olive-green and gray upperparts, bright-yellow underparts and chin, and a bold, white eye ring. Even juveniles are similar, albeit paler. The adult male has a subtle, often-concealed reddish crown patch. Nashville warblers feed on insects and caterpillars, often high in vegetation, and may been seen pumping their tails up and down. Their voice includes repetitive, high-pitched dual notes, likened to *see-it*, followed by a rapid trill. The adult is illustrated.

Northern Parula,

Parula americana
Family Parulidae (Wood-Warblers)
Size: 4.5"
Season: Summer
Habitat: Treetops in woodlands

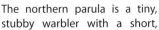

The northern parula is a tiny,
stubby warbler with a short,
sharp bill; short tail; and a relatively large head. Upperparts are
slatey blue with a greenish mantle. Below, there is a white belly
and undertail, a yellow chin and breast, and a rufous breast band,
bordered by dark gray in males. Above and below the eyes are
white eye arcs, and the lower mandible is yellow. The wing shows
two bold, white wing bars. Northern parulas forage for insects
and caterpillars in trees. The adult male is illustrated.

Yellow Warbler,

Dendroica petechia
Family Parulidae (Wood-Warblers)
Size: 5"
Season: Summer
Habitat: Willows and alders near
streamsides, rural shrubbery, gardens

The yellow warbler is widespread
in North America, and sings a
musical *sweet-sweet-sweet*. It is bright yellow overall, with darker
yellow green above and reddish-brown streaking below. The
black eyes stand out on its light face, and the bill is relatively thick
for a warbler. Clean yellow stripes are evident on the fanned tail.
The female is paler overall, with less-noticeable streaking on the
breast and sides. Yellow warblers forage in the brush for insects
and spiders. The adult male is illustrated.

Chestnut-sided Warbler,

Dendroica pensylvanica
Family Parulidae (Wood-Warblers)
Size: 5"
Season: Summer
Habitat: Early-growth forest, shrubby fields, abandoned pasture

The chestnut-sided warbler is a distinctly colored warbler that breeds in New England and often perches with its tail slightly cocked. Adults in summer plumage are streaked black and pale yellow across the back and are white below with a chestnut band along the sides. The head has a bright-yellow crown and a black eye line and moustachial stripe. Females are less chestnut on the sides and less dark on the face. Winter adults are greenish yellow across the back and head with no dark on the face. Chestnut-sided warblers flit through the low understory, gleaning spiders and insects, and sing a series of high, soft notes ending with an accented *wee-choo!* The breeding male (bottom) and nonbreeding male (top) are illustrated.

Magnolia Warbler,

Dendroica magnolia
Family Parulidae (Wood-Warblers)
Size: 4.75"
Season: Summer
Habitat: Coniferous woodlands

The magnolia warbler is a relatively plump, boldly patterned warbler with a longish tail and a short bill. The plumage is medium gray above and bright yellow below and on the rump, with white undertail coverts. The breeding male has a broad black stripe through the face and onto the mantle, and thick, black streaking on the breast and flanks. It also has a white patch at the wing coverts and behind the eye. The nonbreeding male has an all-gray upper head with less-extensive black on the back and breast. Females are somewhat intermediate between breeding and nonbreeding males. Magnolia warblers remain in the cover of vegetation, foraging for insects, and their song is a melody of short, cheery *weet* or *weet-chee* phrases. The breeding male (bottom) and nonbreeding male (top) are illustrated.

Cape May Warbler, *Dendroica tigrina*
Family Parulidae (Wood-Warblers)
Size: 5"
Season: Summer
Habitat: Spruce forests

Breeding across most of Canada and the far northeastern United States, the Cape May warbler is a handsome warbler with a relatively short tail and a thin, blackish bill that has a slight downward curve. Breeding males are olive green above and on the wings, with a broad, white wing patch and white spots on the outer tail feathers. The underparts and head are yellow, with heavy dark streaking on the throat and sides, a dark-gray crown, and reddish-orange auriculars. Females lack the red on the face and are paler overall with a less obvious wing patch. Cape May warblers prefer the upper canopy of spruce or pines, where they feed on insects, especially the spruce budworm. Their voice is a very high-pitched series of clear *see, see, see* notes, or a single *seet*. The breeding male (bottom) and female (top) are illustrated.

Black-throated Blue Warbler, *Dendroica caerulescens*
Family Parulidae (Wood-Warblers)
Size: 5"
Season: Summer
Habitat: Upland woodlands with dense undergrowth

The black-throated blue warbler is a compact, thick-necked warbler with striking sexual dimorphism. The male is steely blue above and white below with a black face, throat, sides, and flanks. The female is drab, olive gray above and pale olive yellow below, with a dark auricular patch and a thin, white supercilium and lower eye-arc. Noticeable in flight or while perched, the white wing patch at the base of the primaries is unique among warblers. They forage primarily for insects in the lower canopy and sing a series of high-pitched, raspy *ze-ze-zhweee* notes, accented and higher at the end. The breeding male (bottom) and female (above) are illustrated.

Yellow-rumped Warbler,

Dendroica coronata
Family Parulidae (Wood-Warblers)
Size: 5.5"
Season: Summer
Habitat: Deciduous and coniferous
woodlands, suburbs

WOOD-WARBLERS

Two races of this species occur in North America: The "myrtle" form ranges across the continent, including New England, and the "Audubon's" form is found west of the Rockies. The myrtle variety is blue gray above, with dark streaks and white below, black streaking below the chin, and a bright-yellow side patch. There is a black mask across the face bordered by a thin superciliary stripe above and a white throat below. The nonbreeding adult and female are paler, with a more brownish cast to the upperparts. The longish tail has white spots on either side and meets with the conspicuous yellow rump. The Audubon's variety has a yellow chin and a gray face. Yellow-rumped warblers prefer to eat berries and insects. The male myrtle form is illustrated.

Black-throated Gray Warbler,

Dendroica nigrescens
Family Parulidae (Wood-Warblers)
Size: 5.5"
Season: Spring and fall migrant
Habitat: Mixed woodlands, chaparral

The black-throated gray warbler is a boldly patterned black-and-white warbler with a relatively thick, pointed bill. It is slate gray above, streaked on the mantle, and has clear white wing bars. Underneath, it is white with black streaks that merge into a black throat, and the outer tail feathers are white. The head has white patches below and above the eyes, and there are yellow loreal patches. The female has less barring underneath. Black-throated gray warblers actively forage through foliage for insects and voice a series of wheezy notes, ascending in volume, sounding like *wee-wee-wee-wee-weet*. The male is illustrated.

Black-throated Green Warbler,
Dendroica virens
Family Parulidae (Wood-Warblers)
Size: 5"
Season: Summer
Habitat: Coniferous and mixed woodlands

The "green" of the black-throated green warbler is restricted to the back, mantle, crown, and patterning about the otherwise bright-yellow face. The wings are dark gray with white wing bars edging the coverts, and the tail is dark gray with white outer retricies. The underparts are white and tinged with yellow, with bold black streaking across the sides. Males have a black throat; females have a whitish throat. These warblers feed high in the canopy for insects or berries and can be detected by their song of buzzy notes like *zee, zee, zee, zoo-ee*. The breeding male is illustrated.

Blackburnian Warbler,
Dendroica fusca
Family Parulidae (Wood-Warblers)
Size: 5"
Season: Summer
Habitat: Mature coniferous or mixed woodlands

The Blackburnian warbler is a beautifully colored and boldly patterned warbler with a relatively large head and neck. The breeding male is black above with extensive white on the wing coverts and whitish streaks on the back. The underside progresses from bright yellow orange on the head and throat to yellow on the breast to white toward the rear. The head has a black crown and facial pattern, and there is black streaking down the sides. The female has similar patterning but is duller overall, with less orange and less white on the wing coverts. Blackburnian warblers perch and forage high in the tree canopy, feeding on insects, and sing a series of extremely high-pitched *tsee* or *sit* notes. The breeding male (bottom) and female (top) are illustrated.

Yellow-throated Warbler,
Dendroica dominica
Family Parulidae (Wood-Warblers)
Size: 5.25"
Season: Summer
Habitat: Coniferous and mixed woodlands near water

The yellow-throated warbler is an elongated, long-billed warbler that forages high in the tree canopy picking insects from the bark. Its plumage is slate gray above and white below, heavily streaked with black, and it has a clean yellow chin and breast. There is a bold face pattern with a white supercilium and lower eye arc bordered by a black eye stripe and auricular area. Behind the ear is a distinctive white patch. The dark back contrasts with two white wing bars. The outer tail feathers show patches of white. The adult is illustrated.

Pine Warbler, *Dendroica pinus*
Family Parulidae (Wood-Warblers)
Size: 5.5"
Season: Summer
Habitat: Pine and mixed pine woodlands

The pine warbler creeps along pine branches picking insects from the bark. It is a rounded, long-winged warbler with a relatively thick bill. Plumage is olive green above with gray wings, and yellow below streaked with olive. Belly and undertail coverts are white. The yellow of the chin extends under the auricular area; a faint "spectacle" is formed by the light lores and eye ring, and there are two clearly marked white wing bars. The female is paler overall, and the juvenile lacks yellow on the chin and underparts. The outer tail feathers show white patches. The illustration shows an adult male.

Prairie Warbler, *Dendroica discolor*
Family Parulidae (Wood-Warblers)
Size: 4.5"
Season: Summer
Habitat: Early succession forests, shrubs

The prairie warbler is a small, plump, long-tailed warbler with a rising, buzzy song, sometimes sung from a treetop perch. It is olive-green above and bright yellow below, with black streaking along its sides topped by a distinct spot just behind the bottom of the chin. A dark half-circle swoops underneath the eye, and sometimes rusty streaking is seen on the mantle. The female is slightly paler overall. The outer tail feathers are white. Prairie warblers forage through low branches of the understory for insects and spiders. The adult male is illustrated.

Palm Warbler, *Dendroica palmarum*
Family Parulidae (Wood-Warblers)
Size: 5.5"
Season: Summer
Habitat: Thickets near spruce bogs, open grassland

The palm warbler forages on the ground for insects while constantly bobbing its tail. It is brownish above with darker streaking, and pale brown-gray below with dark streaking. Chin and undertail coverts are bright yellow. The head has a dark eye stripe, a pale superciliary stripe, and a dark, rufous crown. Nonbreeding adults are paler, with a gray chin and brown crown. Outer tail feathers show small white patches and contrast with an olive-yellow rump. Two races of this species occur: the "yellow," with a yellow underside (present in New England), and the "brown," with a pale-gray belly and brown streaking (ranging farther west). The breeding adult is illustrated.

Bay-breasted Warbler, *Dendroica castanea*
Family Parulidae (Wood-Warblers)
Size: 5.5"
Season: Summer
Habitat: Open coniferous spruce or mixed woodlands

The bay-breasted warbler is a relatively large warbler that breeds in northern boreal forests and winters in tropical South America. Its body is compact with fairly long wingtips and a stout, thick-based bill. The breeding male is pale gray and black above, with prominent, white wing bars and white spots on the outer tail feathers. The belly and sides of the nape are creamy white, the crown, upper breast, and sides are chestnut brown (bay-colored), and the face has a black mask. Breeding females are similar but with less brown on a much paler, grayish face, and more muted brown on the breast and sides. Nonbreeding males are yellow green on the back and head and lack the brown breast. They prefer middle canopy foliage, usually among spruce trees, where they glean for insects, especially the spruce budworm. The voice is a series of high-pitched, loud *see* notes, often accelerating toward the end. The breeding male (bottom) and female (top) are illustrated.

Blackpoll Warbler,

Dendroica townsendi
Family Parulidae (Wood-Warblers)
Size: 5.5"
Season: Summer
Habitat: Spruce and fir forests

The blackpoll warbler is a common
warbler of high-altitude forests that makes a very long migration to wintering grounds in South America. The breeding male is streaked gray and black above with distinct white wing bars; it is white below with black streaking. The head is white on the face and capped with black, and the legs are yellow. Females and nonbreeding males are paler overall, grayish or olive green above, washed with buff or yellowish below, and lacking a dark cap. Blackpoll warblers feed on insects in foliage often high in trees, making them sometimes difficult to spot, and voice extremely high-pitched, dry, repeated *sit* notes. The breeding male (bottom) and breeding female (top) are illustrated.

Black-and-white Warbler,

Mniotilta varia
Family Parulidae (Wood-Warblers)
Size: 5.25"
Season: Summer
Habitat: Mixed woodlands

The black-and-white warbler is a unique warbler that behaves more like a nuthatch, creeping up and down tree trunks probing for insects in the bark with its long, downcurved bill. The breeding male, as its name suggests, is streaked black and white overall, with a black throat, auricular patch, and crown that is topped with a thin white medial stripe. Females have paler streaking on the undersides, a white throat, gray auriculars, and buff flanks. Both sexes have black spotting on the undertail coverts. The voice is a series of high-pitched *see-see-see* notes or a quick *seeta-seeta-seeta*. The breeding male (bottom) and a female (top) are illustrated.

Cerulean Warbler,
Dendroica cerulea
Family Parulidae (Wood-Warblers)
Size: 4.5"
Season: Summer
Habitat: Tall deciduous woodlands near water

The cerulean warbler is a small, somewhat uncommon, short-tailed warbler of the high treetops, whose robust, buzzy warble is often the first indication of its presence. The male is bright cerulean blue above and on the head, white below and on the chin, and has dark gray-blue streaking along the sides, below a thin breast band. Females are pale blue green above with pale streaking below over yellowish-white sides. Cerulean warblers glean insects high in the canopy. The male (bottom) and female (top) are illustrated.

Prothonotary Warbler,
Protonotaria citrea
Family Parulidae (Wood-Warblers)
Size: 5.5"
Season: Summer
Habitat: Wooded swamps

Also known as the golden swamp warbler, the prothonotary warbler is a fairly large warbler with a short tail, a relatively large head, and a long, sharp bill. The head and underparts are a rich yellow to yellow orange, and the undertail coverts are white. The wings and tail are blue gray and there is an olive-green mantle. Females and juveniles are paler overall with an olive cast to the head. Prothonotary warblers forage through the understory for insects. The adult male is illustrated.

Worm-eating Warbler,
Helmitheros vermivorum
Family Parulidae (Wood-Warblers)
Size: 5.25"
Season: Summer
Habitat: Dense growth in woodlands, often near streams

The worm-eating warbler is a plain-looking, relatively large warbler with a short, stubby tail and a thick, long bill. The sexes are similar in plumage, which is olive brown above and pale buff below, with no apparent wing bars or tail spots. The only obvious markings are on the head, which has two thin, black crown stripes and thin, black eye lines. The legs are pale pinkish or flesh-colored. Worm-eating warblers forage on or close to the ground for insects and caterpillars, not necessarily just worms, as the common name would imply. Their song is a rapid trill of dry, toneless, buzzy notes. The adult is illustrated.

Ovenbird, *Seiurus aurocapilla*
Family Parulidae (Wood-Warblers)
Size: 6"
Season: Summer
Habitat: Mature deciduous or mixed woodlands

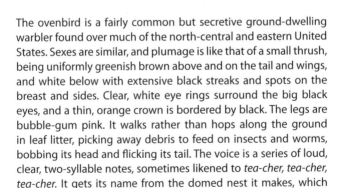

The ovenbird is a fairly common but secretive ground-dwelling warbler found over much of the north-central and eastern United States. Sexes are similar, and plumage is like that of a small thrush, being uniformly greenish brown above and on the tail and wings, and white below with extensive black streaks and spots on the breast and sides. Clear, white eye rings surround the big black eyes, and a thin, orange crown is bordered by black. The legs are bubble-gum pink. It walks rather than hops along the ground in leaf litter, picking away debris to feed on insects and worms, bobbing its head and flicking its tail. The voice is a series of loud, clear, two-syllable notes, sometimes likened to *tea-cher, tea-cher, tea-cher*. It gets its name from the domed nest it makes, which resembles a small Dutch oven. The adult is illustrated.

Wilson's Warbler, *Wilsonia pusilla*
Family Parulidae (Wood-Warblers)
Size: 4.75"
Season: Summer
Habitat: Willow and alder thickets, woodlands near water

The Wilson's warbler is a small, lively warbler with a narrow tail and a short bill. It is uniformly olive green above and yellow below, with some olive-green smudging. The head has large black eyes and a beanie-shaped black cap. Females and juveniles have a greenish cap with variable amounts of black. Wilson's warblers stay low to the ground, gleaning food from the vegetation, or hover and hawk for insects. Their voice is a rapid series of chattering notes, or a quick *chip* call. The adult male is illustrated.

American Redstart,
Setophaga ruticilla
Family Parulidae (Wood-Warblers)
Size: 5"
Season: Summer
Habitat: Open mixed woodlands in early succession

The American redstart is constantly active and frenetic, displaying by fanning its tail and wings while perched. The plumages of males and females are markedly different: The male is jet black above and white below, with a fiery red patch at the side of the breast and a paler, peachy-red wing bar and sides of the tail. The female is gray green above with a slate-gray head and white chin and breast. Its colored areas are located in the same areas as the male but are yellow. Redstarts eat insects gleaned from branches and bark, or hawk for insects. The female (top) and adult male (bottom) are illustrated.

Northern Waterthrush,

Parkesia noveboracensis
Family Parulidae (Wood-Warblers)
Size: 5.75"
Season: Summer
Habitat: Wooded areas near
streamsides, brushy wetlands

Always found close to water, the northern waterthrush is a large warbler (not a thrush) with a long bill and relatively short tail. Both sexes have similar plumage, which is dark brown above and whitish or buff below with brown streaking across the breast, sides, and flanks. The head is patterned with a dark crown, eye stripe, and auricular patch and has a broad white supercilium, malar region, and throat. The legs are long, thin, and pinkish. Waterthrushes forage on stream banks for insects or aquatic invertebrates, habitually bobbing their tails. The Louisiana waterthrush, also found in New England, is almost identical, but it tends to favor faster-running streams than the northern. The adult is illustrated.

Common Yellowthroat,

Geothlypis trichas
Family Parulidae (Wood-Warblers)
Size: 5"
Season: Summer
Habitat: Low vegetation near water,
swamps, fields

The common yellowthroat scampers through the undergrowth looking for insects and spiders in a somewhat wren-like manner. It is a plump little warbler that often cocks up its tail. Its plumage is olive brown above and pale brown to whitish below, with a bright-yellow breast-to-chin region and undertail coverts. The male has a black facial mask trailed by a fuzzy white area on the nape. The female lacks the facial mask. The female (top) and male (bottom) are illustrated.

Hooded Warbler, *Wilsonia citrina*
Family Parulidae (Wood-Warblers)
Size: 5"
Season: Summer
Habitat: Moist woodlands, swamps

The hooded warbler lurks in the woodland understory picking out insects while continually flicking its tail and singing its high, musical *weeta-weeta-weeta-toe.* Plumage is olive green above and bright yellow below. The male has a full, black hood encompassing the face and chin, while the female has a fainter, partial mask with a yellow chin. In the fanned tail one can see white inner vanes to the outer tail feathers. The adult male (bottom) and female (top) are illustrated.

Canada Warbler,
Cardellina canadensis
Family Parulidae (Wood-Warblers)
Size: 5.25"
Season: Summer
Habitat: Deciduous and mixed woodlands with dense, moist underbrush

The Canada warbler is a bright warbler of thick, shady woodlands, breeding not just in Canada but throughout most of the north-eastern United States. Both sexes are lemon yellow below and on the throat, uniformly slate-gray above and on the wings and tail, and have a distinct, complete whitish eye ring and a yellow loreal patch. Males also have black streaking on the breast, forming a neat "necklace," and black at the front half of the face. Females have very limited, lighter streaking on the breast (sometimes nearly absent), no black on the face, and an olive-tinted forehead. The legs are pale yellow to reddish-orange. They forage in the dense understory of trees or tall brush, often cocking their tails, gleaning insects and spiders or catching flying insects near the ground. Their voice is a cheerful, musical warble. The adult male is illustrated.

Eastern Towhee, *Pipilo erythrophthalmus*
Family Emberizidae (Sparrows, Buntings)
Size: 8"
Season: Summer
Habitat: Thickets, suburban shrubs, gardens

The eastern towhee is a large, long-tailed sparrow with a thick, short bill and sturdy legs. It forages on the ground in dense cover by kicking back both feet at once to uncover insects, seeds, and worms. It is black above, including the head and upper breast, and it has rufous sides and a white belly. The base of the primaries is white, as are the corners of the tail. Eye color ranges from red to white, depending on the region. Females are like the males but brown above. Its song is a musical *drink-your-teee*. The eastern towhee was once conspecific with the spotted towhee as the rufous-sided towhee. The adult male is illustrated.

American Tree Sparrow,
Spizella arborea
Family Emberizidae (Sparrows, Buntings)
Size: 6.25"
Season: Winter
Habitat: Open fields with brush or weedy areas

The American tree sparrow is a plump, large-headed, long-tailed winter visitor that breeds in Alaska and the northern latitudes of Canada. The sexes look alike, with a streaked rufous and black back, white wing bars, a pale-gray belly with rufous on the sides, and a single, central, dark spot on the breast. The head is mostly pale gray with a bright rufous crown and eye line, and a thick, stubby bill that is pale orange on the lower mandible and blackish on the upper mandible. American tree sparrows add a cheerful note to the cold New England winters with their musical, high-pitched chattering, as they hop along the ground feeding on grasses and seeds. They also readily visit suburban feeders. The adult is illustrated.

SPARROWS, BUNTINGS

151

Chipping Sparrow,
Spizella passerina
Family Emberizidae (Sparrows,
Buntings)
Size: 5.5"
Season: Summer
Habitat: Dry fields, woodland edges,
gardens

The chipping sparrow is a medium-size sparrow with a slightly notched tail and a rounded crest. The upperparts are barred black and brown with a gray rump, while the underparts are pale gray. The head has a rufous crown, white superciliary stripes, dark eye line, and white throat. The bill is short, conical, and pointed. The sexes are similar, and winter adults are duller and lack the rufous color on the crown. Chipping sparrows feed in trees or on open ground in loose flocks, searching for seeds and insects. Their voice is a rapid, staccato chipping sound. The breeding adult is illustrated.

Field Sparrow, *Spizella pusilla*
Family Emberizidae (Sparrows, Buntings)
Size: 5.75"
Season: Summer
Habitat: Fields with bushy cover or
scattered trees

The field sparrow is a rather slender and plain-colored sparrow with a long, notched tail and a thick-based, stubby, pinkish bill. It is brownish above with dark streaking and pale wing bars, and grayish below with a rufous wash along the breast and flanks. The head is mostly gray with a rufous crown and upper auricular patch, and a distinct, thin, white eye ring. The sexes are similar, while juveniles are duller overall with moderate dark streaking on the breast. Field sparrows forage on the ground and brush for seeds and insects, and sing, often from a conspicuous perch, a series of clear, high notes that gradually increase in speed to a rapid trill. The adult is illustrated.

Vesper Sparrow, *Spizella gramineus*
Family Emberizidae (Sparrows, Buntings)
Size: 6.5"
Season: Summer
Habitat: Pastures, cultivated fields, grasslands

Named for the evening (*vesper*), the time in which it often sings its sweet song, the vesper sparrow is a large sparrow with a medium-size bill and a notched tail. The upperparts are brown with heavy darker streaking and a rufous patch at the shoulder. The underparts are buffy to whitish with dark streaking along the breast and sides. The eyes have a thin, white eye ring, the dark auriculars have a pale interior, and there is a thin malar stripe. In flight the white outer tail feathers are conspicuous. Vesper sparrows feed on or near the ground for insects, seeds, and worms. Their song starts with slow, clear notes followed by rapid trilled notes. The adult is illustrated.

Savannah Sparrow,
Passerculus sandwichensis
Family Emberizidae (Sparrows, Buntings)
Size: 5.5"
Season: Summer
Habitat: A wide variety of open spaces, including grassy fields, meadows, coastal dunes, croplands, and roadsides

The Savannah sparrow is a widespread, common, crisply streaked sparrow with pinkish legs and a relatively short, notched tail. There is much geographical variation in terms of color and darkness of streaking. In general, the upperparts are gray brown to reddish brown and heavily streaked with black. The underparts are white with a pale-brown wash along the sides as well as extensive dark streaking on the sides and breast that often meets to form a loose spot at the center of the breast. The head is brown to gray with a darker crown, eye stripe, and malar stripe, and has a yellowish loreal patch. Savannah sparrows feed by walking or hopping along the ground for insects and seeds. Their song consists of a few dry, high notes followed by a longer trill. The adult is illustrated.

Grasshopper Sparrow,
Ammodramus savannarum
Family Emberizidae (Sparrows, Buntings)
Size: 5"
Season: Summer
Habitat: Grassland with scrub

The grasshopper sparrow has a large, flattened head and a short tail. Above, it is streaked brown, white, and black, while below it is an unstreaked buff. The head is also plain buff with a darkish spot on the cheek and dark crown stripes between a light medial stripe. The sexes are similar, while juveniles show noticeable streaking across the breast and flanks. Grasshopper sparrows feed in grasses or on the ground for grasshoppers (of course!), other insects, and seeds, and may sing from a conspicuous perch a drawn out, thin, buzzy song and short *chip* notes. They often run when alarmed or fly in erratic, weak spurts. The adult is illustrated.

Saltmarsh Sparrow,
Ammodramus caudacutus
Family Emberizidae (Sparrows, Buntings)
Size: 5.25"
Season: Summer
Habitat: Saltwater or freshwater marshes, grasslands

The saltmarsh sparrow is a ground-dwelling, thick-necked sparrow with a flattish crown. The tail is short with pointed feathers, which is where it gets its name. Plumage is streaked brownish above with contrasting white streaks, while the underside is white and heavily streaked, with an orange wash on the sides. The nape is gray, and the crown and auriculars are dark, surrounded by an orange superciliary stripe, ear patches, and malar area. This bird stays low to the ground, even in flight, and quickly dives for cover. It was once considered conspecific with the Nelson's sparrow, as the sharp-tailed sparrow. The adult is illustrated.

Seaside Sparrow,
Ammodramus maritimus
Family Emberizidae (Sparrows, Buntings)
Size: 6"
Season: Year-round
Habitat: Coastal saltwater marshes, freshwater marshes

The seaside sparrow is plump with a relatively large, flat head, a fairly long bill, and a short tail. Plumage is olive brown above with dark streaking, and white below with dark streaks or spots. The chin is white, bordered by an obvious moustachial stripe, and the supraloreal region is yellow. This bird forages among the marsh vegetation for insects, seeds, and small crustaceans and snails. It dives quickly into cover from flight. The adult is illustrated.

Lincoln's Sparrow,
Melospiza lincolnii
Family Emberizidae (Sparrows, Buntings)
Size: 5.75"
Season: Summer
Habitat: Moist areas with shrubs or low trees, marshes, thickets

The Lincoln's sparrow is a skulking, secretive, compact sparrow with a relatively thin bill and a raised crest when alarmed. The upperparts are brownish and streaked with black, while the underparts are buff with fine, dark streaking and a white belly. The head has a rufous crown stripe, gray median crown stripes, a gray supercilium, dark borders above and below the auriculars, and a dark malar stripe. Lincoln's sparrows feed on the ground for insects and seeds, commonly scratching the ground. Their voice is a short, warbling, musical song of buzzy notes and trills. The breeding adult is illustrated.

Song Sparrow, *Melospiza melodia*
Family Emberizidae (Sparrows, Buntings)
Size: 6"
Season: Year-round
Habitat: Thickets, shrubs, woodland edges near water

One of the most common sparrows, the song sparrow is fairly plump and has a long, rounded tail. It is brown and gray above with streaking, and white below with heavy dark or brownish streaking that often congeals into a discrete spot in the middle of the breast. The head has a dark crown with a gray medial stripe, dark eye line, and dark malar stripe above the white chin. Song sparrows are usually seen in small groups or individually, foraging on the ground for insects and seeds. The song is a series of chips and trills of variable pitch, and the call is a *chip-chip-chip*. The adult is illustrated.

Swamp Sparrow,
Melospiza georgiana
Family Emberizidae (Sparrows, Buntings)
Size: 5.75"
Season: Year-round
Habitat: Marshes, pond edges, coastal regions

The swamp sparrow, true to its name, is a denizen of marshes, bogs, and moist thickets, where it voices a repetitive, rather monotone, extended trill of *twee-twee-twee* notes. The plumage is rufous above with black streaking on the back; below it is grayish with faint streaks, a rufous wash along the flanks, and white on the belly. The head has a rufous crown, a dark postocular stripe, and a faint moustachial stripe below a pale, buff-gray malar area and white throat. Swamp sparrows feed on insects, seeds, or aquatic invertebrates. The adult is illustrated.

Fox Sparrow, *Passerella iliaca*
Family Emberizidae (Sparrows, Buntings)
Size: 7"
Season: Year-round
Habitat: Dense thickets in woodland and riparian areas

Of the four varieties of the large, plump, ground-dwelling fox sparrow that occur in North America, the "red" or "taiga" group is the only type found in New England. It is streaked reddish brown and gray above with thin, white wing bars, has a brown tail, and is white below with extensive brown spotting on the breast and sides, sometimes meeting in a heavy blotch at the center of the breast. The head is gray with a reddish crown and auriculars, and the bill is orangey or grayish with a dark line on the top edge. Sexes are similar. Fox sparrows forage on the ground and in thickets for seeds and insects, often scratching back with both feet to uncover food. The voice is a loud, clear collection of rising and falling musical notes. The adult "red" form is illustrated.

White-throated Sparrow,

Zonotrichia albicollis
Family Emberizidae (Sparrows, Buntings)
Size: 6.5"
Season: Year-round
Habitat: Undergrowth of mixed woodlands, thickets, gardens

The white-throated sparrow is a fairly large, rounded sparrow with a long tail and typical short, thick bill. It is brown with dark streaking above, has a gray rump, and is grayish below, washed with brown and lightly streaked. The head has a black crown that is bisected by a white medial strip, a white superciliary stripe with yellow near the lores, and a dark eye line. The white chin is sharply bordered by the gray breast below. White-throated sparrows forage on the ground in small flocks, often with other species, picking up insects and seeds. Their song is a clean, piercing, simple whistle that mimics the phrase *old sam peabody, peabody, peabody*. The adult is illustrated.

White-crowned Sparrow,

Zonotrichia leucophrys
Family Emberizidae (Sparrows, Buntings)
Size: 7"
Season: Spring and fall migrant
Habitat: Brushy areas, woodland edges, gardens

The white-crowned sparrow has a rounded head, sometimes with a raised peak, and a fairly long, slightly notched tail. It is brownish above, streaked on the mantle, and shows pale wing bars. The underside is grayish on the breast, fading to pale brown on the belly and flanks. The head is gray below the eye and boldly patterned black and white above the eye, with a white medial crown stripe. The bill is bright yellow orange. White-crowned sparrows forage on the ground, often in loose flocks, scratching for insects, seeds, and berries. Their song is variable, but it usually starts with one longer whistle followed by several faster notes. The adult is illustrated.

Dark-eyed Junco, *Junco hyemalis*
Family Emberizidae (Sparrows, Buntings)
Size: 6.5"
Season: Year-round
Habitat: Open coniferous and mixed woodlands, thickets, rural gardens

The dark-eyed junco is a small, plump sparrow with a short, conical pink bill and several distinct variations in plumage. The most widespread form, and the only form found in New England, is the "slate-colored." It is slate gray to brownish gray overall with a white belly and undertail coverts, and a pinkish bill. The male is generally grayer, while the female tends to be browner. The white outer tail feathers are obvious in flight. Juncos hop about on the ground, often in groups, picking up insects and seeds. Their voice is a staccato, monotone, chirping trill. The slate-colored adult male is illustrated.

Lapland Longspur,
Calcarius lapponicus
Family Emberizidae (Sparrows, Buntings)
Size: 6.5"
Season: Winter
Habitat: Fields, shorelines

The Lapland longspur is a large, sparrow-like bird that forms enormous flocks during migration or on its wintering grounds. The breeding male is heavily streaked brown, black, and white above, and is white below with thick black streaking on the sides and flanks. The head and upper breast are black, the nape is chestnut, and a white line runs behind the eye and across the neck. Females and nonbreeding males are plainer on the head but show a distinct dark arc on the face. Longspurs are so called because of their elongated rear claws. They feed on the ground for seeds and insects. The nonbreeding male (top) and breeding male (bottom) are illustrated.

Snow Bunting, *Plectrophenax nivalis*
Family Emberizidae (Sparrows, Buntings)
Size: 6.5"
Season: Winter
Habitat: Grassy fields, beaches

The aptly named snow bunting breeds in the highest, coldest latitudes of the Arctic region. Appearing plump due to its dense plumage, it is shaped like most sparrows and has a short bill. The breeding male is white with a black back, wing tips, central tail area, legs, bill, and eyes. Breeding females are similar but with grayish smudging on the face, nape, and crown, and paler, browner markings on the back. Nonbreeding adults are washed with rusty brown. Snow buntings forage on the ground for insects and seeds and voice a somewhat raspy, musical warble. The nonbreeding male (top) and breeding male (bottom) are illustrated.

Scarlet Tanager, *Piranga olivacea*
Family Cardinalidae (Cardinals, Grosbeaks, Tanagers, Buntings)
Size: 7"
Season: Summer
Habitat: Leafy deciduous forests, suburban parks

The scarlet tanager is a secretive bird of the high canopy that is often detected first by its voice, despite its bright plumage. The breeding male is rich scarlet red overall with contrasting black wings and tail. Females and nonbreeding males are similar, colored olive yellow above and yellow below, with dark wings and tail. Males in fall molt show a patchwork of yellow, green, and red feathers. Scarlet tanagers feed on insects, spiders, and berries at the upper levels of large trees and sing a series of raspy, quick phrases, comparable to that of a robin. The breeding (bottom) and nonbreeding (top) males are illustrated.

Northern Cardinal, *Cardinalis cardinalis*
Family Cardinalidae (Cardinals, Grosbeaks, Tanagers, Buntings)
Size: 8.5"
Season: Year-round
Habitat: Woodlands with thickets, suburban gardens

The northern cardinal, with its thick, powerful bill, eats mostly seeds but will also forage for fruit and insects. It is often found in pairs and is quite common at suburban feeders. It is a long-tailed songbird with a thick, short, orange bill and a tall crest. The male is red overall with a black mask and chin. The female is brownish above, dusky below, and crested, with a dark front to the face. Juveniles are similar to the female but have a black bill. The voice is a musical *weeta-weeta* or *woit* heard from a tall, exposed perch. The adult male (bottom) and adult female (top) are illustrated.

Rose-breasted Grosbeak,
Pheucticus ludovicianus
Family Cardinalidae (Cardinals, Grosbeaks, Tanagers, Buntings)
Size: 8.25"
Season: Summer
Habitat: Deciduous or mixed woodlands, especially near dense shrub and water

The rose-breasted grosbeak is a chunky but lovely finch-like songbird with a relatively large head and a huge, conical bill. The breeding male is black on the head, wings, back, and tail, with contrasting white on the rump, outer retrices, and wing coverts. The underside is white with a brilliant, rose-colored breast. Females are quite different: dark brown above, white below with extensive streaking, and a boldly patterned white and brown face. Rose-breasted grosbeaks usually remain high in the canopy, feeding on a variety of insects, seeds, and fruits, and sing a cheery, musical, meandering song. The adult male (bottom) and a female (top) are illusrated.

Indigo Bunting, *Passerina cyanea*
Family Cardinalidae (Cardinals, Grosbeaks, Tanagers, Buntings)
Size: 5.5"
Season: Summer
Habitat: Brush, open woodlands, fields

Often occurring in large flocks, the indigo bunting forages mostly on the ground for insects, berries, and seeds. It is a compact, small songbird with a short, thick bill. The male is entirely blue; the head is a dark, purplish blue and the body is a lighter, sky blue. The female is brownish gray above, duller below, with faint streaking on the breast meeting a white throat. The winter male is smudged with patchy gray, brown, and white. They perch in treetops voicing their undulating, chirping melodies. The adult male (bottom) and female (top) are illustrated.

Bobolink, *Dolichonyx oryzivorus*
Family Icteridae (Blackbirds, Grackles, Orioles)
Size: 7"
Season: Summer
Habitat: Lush prairies, grasslands, agricultural areas

The bobolink is shaped like an elongated sparrow with pointy wings and exhibits quite different plumage in males and females. The female and winter male are a buff brown overall and paler below, with streaking along the back and sides. On the face is a thin, dark crown and eye stripe. The breeding male is white above and black below, with a two-toned head that is black in front and light yellow in back. The bobolink's song is a playful, jumbled melody that some compare to its name, *bobolink-bobolink*. The female (top) and breeding male (bottom) are illustrated.

Red-winged Blackbird,
Agelaius phoeniceus
Family Icteridae (Blackbirds, Grackles, Orioles)
Size: 8.5"
Season: Summer
Habitat: Marshes, meadows, agricultural areas near water

The red-winged blackbird is a widespread, ubiquitous, chunky meadow dweller that forms huge flocks during the nonbreeding season. The male is deep black overall with bright-orange-red lesser coverts and pale medial coverts that form an obvious shoulder patch in flight but may be partially concealed on the perched bird. The female is barred tan and dark brown overall with a pale superciliary stripe and malar patch. Red-winged blackbirds forage marshland for insects, spiders, and seeds. Their voice is a loud, raspy, vibrating *konk-a-leee* given from a perch atop a tall reed or branch. The female (top) and male (bottom) are illustrated.

Eastern Meadowlark, *Sturnella magna*
Family Icteridae (Blackbirds, Grackles, Orioles)
Size: 9.5"
Season: Summer
Habitat: Open fields, grasslands, meadows

The eastern meadowlark is a chunky, short-tailed icterid with a flat head and a long, pointed bill. It is heavily streaked and barred above, and yellow beneath with dark streaking. The head has a dark crown, a white superciliary stripe, a dark eye line, and a yellow chin. On the upper breast is a black, V-shaped necklace that becomes quite pale during winter months. Meadowlarks gather in loose flocks to pick through the grass for insects and seeds. They often perch on telephone wires or posts to sing their short, whistling phrases. The illustration shows a breeding adult.

165

Rusty Blackbird, *Euphagus carolinus*
Family Icteridae (Blackbirds, Grackles, Orioles)
Size: 9"
Season: Summer
Habitat: Marshes, riversides, pastures near water

The rusty blackbird is a sleek, medium-size blackbird that resembles the Brewer's blackbird, whose range is farther west. The breeding male is matte black overall with a contrasting pale-yellow eye. The winter male is dark but barred with rusty brown along the back and breast and has a mostly brown head except for the lores and auricular area. The winter female is paler still, with lighter brown above and on the head, and has a grayish rump. Rusty blackbirds feed in small flocks in shallow water for aquatic invertebrates or in nearby fields for seeds. Their song is a series of chattery, squeaky, jumbled notes accented at the end with a louder, high-pitched *ee*. Once quite abundant, its numbers have decreased dramatically in recent years. The breeding male (bottom) and female (top) are illustrated.

Common Grackle, *Quiscalus quiscula*
Family Icteridae (Blackbirds, Grackles, Orioles)
Size: 12.5"
Season: Summer
Habitat: Pastures, open woodlands, urban parks

The common grackle is a large blackbird with an elongated body, a long, heavy bill, and long tail, which is fatter toward the tip and is often folded into a keel shape. Plumage is overall black with a metallic sheen of purple on the head and brown on the wings and underside. The eyes are a contrasting light-yellow color. Quite social, grackles form huge flocks with other blackbirds and forage on the ground for just about any kind of food, including insects, grains, refuse, and crustaceans. The voice is a high-pitched, rasping trill. The adult male is illustrated.

Brown-headed Cowbird,
Molothrus ater
Family Icteridae (Blackbirds, Grackles, Orioles)
Size: 7.5"
Season: Summer
Habitat: Woodland edges, pastures with livestock, grassy fields

The brown-headed cowbird is a stocky, short-winged, short-tailed blackbird with a short, conical bill. The male is glossy black overall with a chocolate-brown head but is sometimes much lighter in western populations. The female is light brown overall with faint streaking on the underparts and a pale throat. Cowbirds often feed in flocks with other blackbirds, picking seeds and insects from the ground, and their voice is a number of gurgling, squeaking phrases. They practice brood parasitism, whereby they lay their eggs in the nests of other passerine species that then raise their young. Hence, their presence often reduces the populations of other songbirds. The dark adult male is illustrated.

Orchard Oriole, *Icterus spurius*
Family Icteridae (Blackbirds, Grackles, Orioles)
Size: 7"
Season: Summer
Habitat: Orchards, open woodlands, parks

The orchard oriole is a small oriole with a relatively thin, short bill and a short tail that it often tilts sideways. The male is black above with a red rump and a black, hooded head. The underside is red-dish or orange brown with a similarly colored shoulder patch. The lower mandible is light blue gray. Females are markedly different, being greenish gray above and bright yellow below with two white wing bars. The juvenile is similar to the female but has a black chin and lores. Orchard orioles feed in trees for insects, fruit, and nectar and emit high, erratic, musical whistles and chirps. The adult male (bottom) and adult female (top) are illustrated.

Baltimore Oriole, *Icterus galbula*
Family Icteridae (Blackbirds, Grackles, Orioles)
Size: 8.5"
Season: Summer
Habitat: Deciduous woodlands, suburban gardens, parks

The Baltimore oriole is a somewhat stocky icterid with a short, squared tail and a straight, tapered bill. The male is bright yellow orange with a black hood. Wings are black with white edging to the flight feathers and coverts and a yellow-orange shoulder patch. The tail is orange with black along the base and down the middle. The female is paler along the sides with a white shoulder patch and a mottled, yellow-and-brown head and plain tail. It forages for insects, fruit, and nectar from the leafy canopy. It is sometimes considered, with Bullock's oriole, as one species, the northern oriole. The adult male (bottom) and adult female (top) are illustrated.

Purple Finch, *Carpodacus purpureus*
Family Fringillidae (Finches)
Size: 6"
Season: Year-round
Habitat: Open coniferous and mixed woodlands, rural gardens and parks

The purple finch is a sturdy, large-headed finch with a short, notched tail and a thick, conical bill. The male is brownish red above with brown streaking, and whitish below with dusky or pink streaking. The head and breast are not purple but rosy red, and there is pale feathering at the base of the bill. Females and juveniles are brownish and heavily streaked, with noticeably darker facial markings on the crown, auricular, and malar region. Purple finches forage in small groups in trees or on the ground for seeds and insects. Their voice is a long, jumbled song of high whistles, cheeps, and trills. The adult female (top) and adult male (bottom) are illustrated.

House Finch, *Carpodacus mexicanus*
Family Fringillidae (Finches)
Size: 6"
Season: Year-round
Habitat: Woodland edges, urban areas

The house finch is a western species that was introduced to eastern North America and is now common and widespread across the country. It is a relatively slim finch with a longish, slightly notched tail and a short, conical bill with a downcurved culmen. The male is brown above with streaking on the back, while below it is pale with heavy streaking. An orange-red wash pervades the supercilium, throat, and upper breast. The female is a drab gray brown, with similar streaking on the back and underside and no red on the face or breast. House finches have a variable diet that includes seeds, insects, and fruit, and they are often the most abundant birds at feeders. Their voice is a rapid, musical warble. The adult male is illustrated.

Red Crossbill, *Loxia curvirostra*
Family Fringillidae (Finches)
Size: 6.25"
Season: Year-round
Habitat: Coniferous forests

True to its name, the red crossbill has a thick, curved bill with
mandibles that cross each
other at the tip. It is a stocky,
large-headed finch with a
short, notched tail and short legs. Males can vary from dull orange
to reddish overall, while females are grayish yellow or pale yellow
green. Both sexes have dark wings that lack obvious wing bars.
Juveniles are light gray with extensive streaking on the head and
underparts. Their unique bill allows them to extract seeds from
pinecones, but they also eat berries and buds. The female (top)
and male (bottom) are illustrated.

FINCHES

White-winged Crossbill,
Loxia leucoptera
Family Fringillidae (Finches)
Size: 6.5"
Season: Year-round
Habitat: Coniferous forests

The white-winged crossbill is a
chunky finch with stubby legs and
a proportionately smaller head and
thinner bill than that of the red
crossbill. Adult males have a rosy-red to pinkish body and head,
with pale-gray lower flanks and black lores. The wings and tail
are black, and there are two prominent white wing bars (giving it
the common name). Females have greenish-yellow to olive-gray
bodies suffused overall with brownish or gray streaking. White-
winged crossbills use their unusual, curving, crossed mandibles to
extract seeds from cones, typically those of fir, spruce, and hem-
lock. Their song consists of quick, chattering high notes and trills.
The female (top) and male (bottom) are illustrated.

Pine Grosbeak, *Pinicola enucleator*
Family Fringillidae (Finches)
Size: 9"
Season: Year-round
Habitat: Coniferous forests in mountainous areas

The pine grosbeak is a sluggish "winter finch" with a long, slightly notched tail and a large, short bill with a curved culmen and hooked tip. The male is rosy red with dark wings that have white wing bars and white-edged tertials. Its sides, flanks, and lower midbelly are grayish, and there is a pale patch of gray below the eye and a minimal dark eye line. Females are mostly gray with a light-olive-green wash across the head, breast, and back. Pine grosbeaks eat berries, buds, and seeds and may visit feeders, where they prefer sunflower seeds. Their song is a series of fluty, warbling notes. The female (top) and male (bottom) are illustrated.

FINCHES

American Goldfinch,

Spinus tristis
Family Fringillidae (Finches)
Size: 5"
Season: Year-round
Habitat: Open fields, marshes, urban feeders

The American goldfinch is a small, cheerful, social finch with a short, notched tail and a small, conical bill. In winter it is brownish gray, lighter underneath, with black wings and tail. There are two white wing bars, and bright yellow on the shoulders, around the eyes, and along the chin. In breeding plumage the male becomes light yellow across the back, underside, and head and develops a black forehead and loreal area, and the bill becomes orange. Females look similar to the winter males. American goldfinches forage by actively searching for insects and seeds of all kinds, particularly thistle seeds. Their voice is a meandering, musical warble that includes high *cheep* notes. The breeding female (top) and breeding male (bottom) are illustrated.

Common Redpoll, *Carduelis flammea*
Family Fringillidae (Finches)
Size: 5.25"
Season: Winter
Habitat: Thickets, mixed woodlands, urban areas

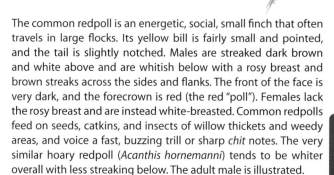

The common redpoll is an energetic, social, small finch that often travels in large flocks. Its yellow bill is fairly small and pointed, and the tail is slightly notched. Males are streaked dark brown and white above and are whitish below with a rosy breast and brown streaks across the sides and flanks. The front of the face is very dark, and the forecrown is red (the red "poll"). Females lack the rosy breast and are instead white-breasted. Common redpolls feed on seeds, catkins, and insects of willow thickets and weedy areas, and voice a fast, buzzing trill or sharp *chit* notes. The very similar hoary redpoll (*Acanthis hornemanni*) tends to be whiter overall with less streaking below. The adult male is illustrated.

Pine Siskin, *Carduelis pinus*
Family Fringillidae (Finches)
Size: 5"
Season: Year-round
Habitat: Coniferous woodlands, rural gardens

The pine siskin is a small, cryptically colored finch with a short tail and a narrow, pointed bill. The head and back are light brown overall and heavily streaked with darker brown. The underside is whitish and streaked darker. There is a prominent yellow wing bar on the greater coverts, and yellow also appears on the flight-feather edges and base of the primaries. Females are marked similarly, with a darker underside and white—not yellow—wing bar. Individuals can be quite variable as to the amount of streaking and prominence of yellow coloring. Pine siskins forage energetically in small groups for seeds and insects, sometime clinging upside down to reach food. Their voice consists of high-pitched, erratic, raspy chips and trills. The adult male is illustrated.

Evening Grosbeak, *Coccothraustes vespertinus*
Family Fringillidae (Finches)
Size: 8"
Season: Year-round
Habitat: Coniferous or mixed woodlands, rural gardens

The evening grosbeak is a comical-looking finch with a large head, a short stubby tail, and an enormous conical bill. In the male, plumage fades from dark brown on the head to bright yellow toward the rump and belly. The wings are black with large white patches on the secondaries and tertials. The yellow superciliums merge with the flat forehead and meet the pale-yellow-green bill. The legs are short and pinkish. Females are grayish overall with choppy white markings on the wings. Evening grosbeaks travel in flocks to feed on seeds and berries in the upper canopy and often visit feeders, preferring sunflower seeds. The voice is a series of short, spaced, rattling *cheep* notes. The female (top) and adult male (bottom) are illustrated.

House Sparrow, *Passer domesticus*
Family Passeridae (Old World Sparrows)
Size: 6.25"
Season: Year-round
Habitat: Urban environments, rural pastures

Introduced from Europe, the house sparrow is ubiquitous in almost every city in the United States and is often the only sparrow-type bird seen in urban areas. It is stocky, aggressive, and gregarious, and has a relatively large head and a short, finch-like bill. Males are streaked brown and black above and are pale below. The lores, chin, and breast are black, while the crown and auriculars are gray. There are prominent white wing bars at the median coverts. In winter the male lacks the dark breast patch. Females are drab overall with a lighter bill and a pale supercilium. House sparrows have a highly varied diet, including grains, insects, berries, and crumbs from the local cafe. Their voice is a series of rather unmusical chirps. The breeding female (top) and breeding male (bottom) are illustrated.

Index

About the Author/Illustrator

Todd Telander is a naturalist/ illustrator/artist who lives in Walla Walla, Washington. He has studied and illustrated wildlife since 1989 while living in California, Colorado, New Mexico, and Washington. He graduated from the University of California, Santa Cruz, with degrees in biology, environmental studies, and scientific illustration, and has since illustrated numerous books and other publications, including FalconGuides' Scats and Tracks series. His wife, Kirsten Telander, is a writer, and they have two sons, Miles and Oliver. His work can be viewed online at toddtelander.com.